Encounters

with Steve de Shazer and Insoo Kim Berg

Inside Stories of
Solution-Focused Brief Therapy

solutions
books

Published in Great Britain in 2015 by
Solutions Books
15 St Georges Avenue
London
N7 0HB
United Kingdom
www.solutionsbooks.com

Bulk sales enquiries (10 copies or more) should be addressed to: Solutions Books via info@sfwork.com or by post to the address above.

ISBN 978-0-9933463-0-9

Design, typesetting and production by
Action Publishing Technology Ltd, Gloucester
Cover design by
Cathi Stevenson

Contents

Brevity of speech gives room for thought.

Jean Paul (1763–1825)

Preface

Bremen, Helsinki, Vienna – these and many other cities, institutes and facilities were among the haunts of Insoo Kim Berg and Steve de Shazer. Throughout the world, and particularly in Europe, these two figures have brought together, inspired and enthused many, many people. Through their travels powerful spiritual connections as well as very real and specific networks have emerged. The annual conferences of the European Brief Therapy Association (EBTA, founded in 1994) are good examples of the established and increasing interdependence of active solution-focused practitioners. Insoo and Steve still speak after their deaths, not only through their articles and books but also in current conversation, thanks to personal memories, anecdotes and stories – for us and many other colleagues. We are, therefore, happy to be close to these pioneers of solution-focused brief therapy in the various contributions published here. Enjoy meeting Insoo and Steve!

Dr. Manfred Vogt
Dr. Ferdinand Wolf
Heinrich Dreesen
Peter Sundman

About the editors

Manfred Vogt from Bremen, at the North German Institute for Short-Term Therapy, NIK, Ferdinand Wolf from Hornstein, Heinrich Dreesen from Bremen, also at the North German Institute for Short-Term Therapy, NIK, and Peter Sundman from Helsinki, at the TaitoBa Institute, have been working for over 20 years as solution-focused brief therapists in private practice and as supervisors and trainers in education and training in Europe and overseas. They worked closely together with Steve and Insoo for over two decades and are founding members and Board Members of the European Brief Therapy Association, EBTA.

Arild Aambø   Oslo, Norway

Keep it clean and simple!

When I first asked Insoo if she would be interested in coming to Norway to teach solution focused therapy, her answer was a blunt: "Norway? No! Never again!" Later I got to know her reasons for this rather surprising answer. She had been in Norway twice before. First she had come with her first husband, who was of Norwegian descent. The couple had wanted to see his family, who lived in a small house in a very remote area on the west coast – a house situated by a desolate road winding along a dark and narrow fiord; on one side the steep rock, on the other just deep water. However picturesque such a fiord may look on post cards, for Insoo it felt like a prison. Any movement outdoors was restricted to the road, and after a couple of days she felt she could not take it any longer. She had more or less dragged herself through the rest of the stay, suffering. The second time she had been invited with Steve to give a seminar on solution focused therapy at a hospital in Oslo. This was right after this therapy form had been introduced to a wider audience and, promising as it was, some people at the hospital wanted to use the opportunity to challenge the approaches that had traditionally been in use at the hospital. As a result, Insoo and Steve soon felt trapped in a harrowing discussion stemming from an ongoing local conflict. That was the last thing they wanted, and when the seminar finally was over, they had promised themselves: "Never again Norway!" However, when Insoo learned about our new project where we wanted to educate a very professionally diverse group of helpers – people working in the home care services, nurses, general practitioners, psychologists and psychiatrists – in solution focused work, thus introducing the method as a kind of common language allowing everybody to collaborate sensitively and effectively with alcohol and drug abusers, she could not resist. Thus we embarked on a long term project during which she visited Oslo again and again. And after this project she continued to visit Oslo and Norway, working with an increasing number of teams and groups.

Nimble and agile as she was, Insoo was very fond of physical activity. She loved tai chi, and she would not even dissociate herself from pushing iron. Privately we got to know that back home during winter she used to get up very early in the morning and go skiing in Milwaukee's biggest park. Taking her at her word, a mutual friend of ours and I invited her to his lodge in the Norwegian mountains where we went skiing. It was a cold, windy winter day and the terrain was quite demanding – something completely different from the parks in Milwaukee. It is not unfair to say that Insoo struggled, trying to make the best out of a pair of borrowed skis and equipment that was not the most adequate. However, that trip turned out to be one out of several times where Insoo really impressed me, not because of her dexterity in skiing, but because of her remarkable endurance. She went on, struggling but never complaining, patiently putting one foot in front of the other, step by step, until we again reached the lodge. Safe in the warm mountain inn she just fell asleep, exhausted, while my friend and I wondered where her stamina and staying power came from. And now we could see the same perseverance in her work and especially in her conversations, where she often kept on asking the same question over and over, never as a routine, always full of wonder.

Becoming more close friends, I was invited to Milwaukee to stay with Insoo and Steve and do some work at the centre. American language was at the time very difficult for me, especially when the clients spoke with an accent, which many of them did – probably because the centre was located just at the border of maybe the least affluent area of Milwaukee and many if not most of the clients had few opportunities to normalise their language through extensive schooling. Nevertheless I was immediately thrown into the therapy room, Insoo herself sitting behind the mirror. "You just have to do it! It's the only way to learn!" she said. And of course she was right. Then after some intense sessions she invited everybody to lunch at the office. She just spread a tablecloth on the floor, placed all the food in the middle, and everybody had to help themselves as best they could. "It's easier to talk like this", Insoo said. "The atmosphere is more relaxed and words come easier". She was right again: there was, already then, a movement from co-evolution or co-construction to co-acting and sensorimotor attunement as a sound basis for languaging.

However, my greatest experience in Milwaukee was perhaps when Steve asked me to cook dinner with him. He knew about my ongoing projects on health promotion activities among immigrants in Oslo – that is, arranging cooking courses on traditional Indian and Pakistani food for health professionals – and he certainly liked to challenge me. While he was preparing for stir frying, he assigned to me to prepare the raw material. And I was not left without instructions: preparing the chicken breast I had to remove everything that had the slightest character of a sinew, and from the broccoli I had to remove all the small stalks which usually emerged where the branches divided. I knew he had refined taste not only in jazz and classical music, but when it came to Japanese wood cuts, beer and food as well. I shared his interests, but these peculiarities that he now demanded from me I had never paid any attention to before. However, I was amazed at his seriousness in the matter: "We have to remove them or they will stick between our teeth!" he kept on saying. I did as he told me, and only slowly did I come to the understanding that this might perhaps be his way of teaching me – in his very personal way – the meaning of Ockham's razor, a matter that obviously was very important for him.

There are of course many, many episodes that come to mind when embarking on a narrative like this, from touring in the Rocky Mountains – where I in sheer distraction left my airplane ticket in my hotel room and Insoo, with her characteristic sense for practical solutions, arranged for it to be sent by courier to our next destination where it actually arrived before us – to giving seminars together or getting valuable help in preparing for conferences and papers. These kinds of experiences really changed my way of thinking, both regarding life in general and especially about what went on in the therapy room. Just a couple of examples: giving seminars with Steve, he refused any kind of planning. "We have to wing it! It's the only way we can be in touch with the audience. Then talk about whatever you like, but leave the miracle question to me!" he would say. Another example: when I suggested as a title for a paper of mine *Creating a common understanding,* Insoo at once suggested, "Would it not be better to call this *Creative use of misunderstandings?*" It was more or less the same thing, and yet I got a completely new understanding about what I had written. A whole new world opened up. I loved her thoughtful comments. At a certain point I was so influenced by Insoo's thinking that when experiencing trouble I started to ask myself, "Suppose Insoo were here, what would she do?" Then it was like a miracle happened; the solution emerged, seemingly from nowhere, took on shape and materialised in time and space. Mysticism? No. Today we have well-grounded scientific work that provides completely adequate explanations for this, but that is another story. The relevant question here is, "What kind of bearing do these episodes have on my understanding of Solution Focused Brief Therapy?" I will just mention a few things that have become important for me, well knowing that Insoo and Steve were both great personalities whose personal commitment shone through any use of method and enriched every relationship they engaged in. In the following, these insights from this couple take the form of some advice:

- Adjust to other people
- Keep it clean and simple
- Remove everything that can disturb the tasteful, flowing, melting, immediate experience
- Be practical and helpful
- Don't give up easily
- Enjoy excellence.

Arild Aambø MD, physician, Oslo, Norway, Senior Consultant NAKMI – Norwegian Research Center for Minority Health.

Corina Ahlers   Vienna, Austria

Memories of Steve and Insoo

My introduction to the solution-oriented scene

In 1985 I was working as a psychologist for the fifth year in an urban psychiatric hospital. Two years previously I had completed a family therapy training, which at that time was dominated by Virginia Satir's humanistic resource model. Personal growth and improvement of self-esteem were the top priorities. In addition, the Milan approach to concepts of circularity and recursion flourished, as did Keeney's ideas regarding the aesthetic use of therapeutic maps. Ancestral delegations to families or couples, the method of family sculpture and the therapeutic treatment of reproachful, rationalising, irrelevant or reassuring communication styles influenced my therapeutic thinking. The primary goal of this largely humanistic, systemic mind-set was to achieve a congruent communication in a family atmosphere for the clients so that their personal growth and sense of worth is promoted.

In 1986 I switched from psychiatry to the prestigious Institute of Family Therapy of Vienna and was able to apply what I had learned about systemics in a new setting. The Institute on the bustling Praterstrasse transported me away from the walls of residential psychiatry. The stigmatised gave way to the ordinary, no more smell of disinfectant and no vistas of cold day rooms with white coats; instead, a shopping street with a McDonald's and an ice cream shop on the ground floor. As a professional coming from in-patient, chronic psychiatry, this new world immersed me in a sea of impressions which, unlike the routines on the psychiatric station, finally intimated therapeutic possibilities. At the Institute, behind the one-way mirror I felt like someone on a safari adventure: families in the wild, me in the bulletproof jeep. I observed the family system, indulged in "system identification" in the Satir sense, (a diagnostic assignment of families based on communication style and self-worth scores) and extended my expert knowledge so that I could work at the Institute with a good conscience, not only behind but also in front of the one-way mirror.

I was proud to belong to the founders of the Austrian Association for Systemic Therapy and Systemic Studies (ÖAS). We understood ourselves as an interdisciplinary scientific platform for discussion where specific systemic distinctions from biology, anthropology, philosophy and therapy were allowed to meet and co-mingle. We watched films by a student of Konrad Lorenz (Professor Schleidt) about fighting turkeys and, in the spirit of Bateson, tried to translate the interactive character of such recursions to a therapeutic session. Although it was nearly impossible with the turkeys, everyone shared the euphoria of Bertallanfy's systems theory until we were duped by the move to constructivism. Having taken second-order cybernetics on board, we learned to focus on the observer's eye and to pay more heed to the internal construction than to the external representations of reality. It was, then, as an initiate teaching therapist at the ÖAS that I first met Steve de Shazer and Insoo Kim Berg. Despite the beautiful surroundings of their workshops, my first impression of them was not very encouraging; Steve de Shazer did not belong in Schloss Neuwaldegg. A grumpy 'Grummelbart' (grumble-beard), his mumbled American was almost impossible to understand. The video of a session with a black client that was shown to the participants, aside from the "Hmm" and "Yeah" after every other second question from Insoo, was completely incomprehensible. Elsewhere in the video, he replied with "I don't know". These gurus insisted that the client, or "visitor" as they preferred, left after the hour visibly relieved, and – just imagine – came again. I could not understand what was supposed to be so extraordinary about this one session.

In Insoo I saw the exotic element that piqued my curiosity and, for me, she was a better teacher than Steve, even though she stayed in his shadow. Moreover, I found the two together as a couple strangely distant, each for himself and yet together.

I was not convinced by these so-called champions of a new systemic school, and after this first introduction I remained sceptical and curious.

However, in 1988 when I was planning my US trip, I knew that the two of them had to be on my itinerary. In the meantime I realised that colleagues held the pair in high esteem, regarded their method as ingenious, and, simply put, found their suggestions to be very helpful for systemic practice. So I wrote a long letter to them and to my hero Harry Goolishian informing them of my intention to tour America systemically. And lo and behold – both Harry Goolishian and Steve de Shazer and Insoo Kim Berg invited me to visit them.

I had not expected that at all. I stayed with both of them and observed them on the job over a 10-day period. The profound differences between Harry in Texas and Steve and Insoo in Milwaukee I can still recall today. First, I visited Harry Goolishian in Galveston and then went on to Milwaukee. Harry's team knew that I planned to visit Steve and Insoo and bade me farewell with the words, "When you arrive, give them a tin of baked beans". To this day, I still have no idea what they meant. Slightly derogatory, ironic, humorous, those parting words are possibly indicative of the slight competition between the two institutions which never got on, preferring to avoid each other.

Personally, I profited enormously from the difference between the two schools: the ambiguity of the extremely hospitable team in Houston collided with the pragmatic, logical brief therapy approach. The masters in Milwaukee were more proficient, effective, visible, Nordic. Since I myself grew up in Spain and live in Austria, I can appreciate these differences and make the most of them.

From Galveston to Milwaukee

In Houston I board the plane and arrive in Milwaukee late in the evening. Steve picks me up, mumbling under his breath a muffled "welcome" and takes me home. Insoo receives me more kindly, shows me my room, then we drink a beer. They love to talk of Europe where, they say, they are better understood than in their own country. Europeans are used to "thinking". What glorious praise for someone who's just come from the old world to the USA.

The two often travel to different places, following invitations, and then meet up here in Milwaukee, as now, in the summer. And this time together is important to get new ideas. It is also the time when many visitors come. They can also benefit from so many people with so many different ways of thinking, but some respite from all the travelling also does them good, the two masters explain. My travel fatigue coupled with their own tiredness means that we soon say goodnight; their terse parting statement: "Tomorrow you'll just come along with us".

My first day at BFTC in Milwaukee

A quick breakfast, a short briefing for the day between the two of them and we drive to the office. Upon arrival I am left to myself, but everything is open and accessible, many people are running around, they answer any questions, are very friendly, and I quickly find the room behind the one-way mirror. A pleasant reminder for me: bulletproof Jeep!

In the Brief Therapy Center the visitor room is situated between two one-way mirrors so that you can look into two different therapy rooms, but audio transmission only works for the main therapy room. So you sit, watching two therapy sessions in parallel, but listening only to one session, until you are distracted by someone bringing in grilled chicken from the Chinese restaurant next door. You eat, seated behind the mirror, because you are hungry and there is never time to eat. Everyone wants to make the most of the time allotted to them: a climate of effectiveness binds us all together. There is a hustle and bustle of people who have never met. They drop in when they are in town, some stay an hour or two behind the mirror, then go again. Nobody has a clear idea of who is coming or going. The mood among the observers behind the one-way mirror is marked by respect and appreciation for each other and the clients. Some want to talk with the masters, others do not. Steve raves about an electrical engineer who has just asked the right questions, because he was not intellectually handicapped from previous therapies. His suggestions would be most useful to Steve when creating the "Central Map" (de Shazer, 1988) for conducting a therapy session!

I am puzzled by this statement. How can Steve trust an engineer, a technician who has nothing to do with matters of the psyche? Even as I ask myself this question, I become aware of my professional prejudices. I have been riding the constructivist wave for a while now and know that this view exists in my head and is not a reality. And I really have no idea how an electrical engineer views matters, because I've never dealt with this before. So maybe, I conclude after some successful self-reflection, I should summon up more curiosity. I realise that it's Steve's gift to astonish people so profoundly that this astonishment can only be assuaged by deep reflection.

I'm also learning how the American lifestyle harmonises with solution-focused therapy. You "go for a walk" around the block or you "do something else". These are the simple tasks set by this form of therapy; they may sound banal to Europeans, but they are everyday activities and thus are meaningful. It's about actions, not interpretations. The brilliant strategy of the two masters combines thinking with doing so that what is essential can emerge and gain importance, helping to promote change and reach the goal. People change without realising it by noticing what they do and interpreting it differently from before. Only after I get back to Vienna and pore over de Shazer's books can I savour the atmosphere and mood at BFTC and associate it with the concepts of "arbitrary" or "involuntary" (de Shazer, 1985).

Suddenly, I reflect about meaning differently: words play with us and we play with words. It is a dance that is moving towards the solution. We therapists want to win this game, but the clients want it too. We have to be able to win them over to a joint work project. In a way, Steve and Insoo invite their clients to join in a game; the game could be entitled "let's invite the solution together." Here there are no losers, only winners or bystanders. Those who look on discover no benefits for themselves, but they watch and observe that others are benefiting. Possibly they will warm to the proposed solution. The game is repeated constantly, and similar patterns emerge from the playful combination of words. A hundred formulations for the same thing, a jazz tune with many variations. The melody will eventually be heard, no one can abandon the game. The therapeutic spirit that pervades and dominates this process declares "there is nothing beyond the solution".

Years later, Steve chooses one of those hundred formulations for a solution in his answer to a question that Hedwig Wagner and I had deliberately kept for him. During a therapy session with a severely depressed client, the client had responded to the miracle question with "the miracle would be that I no longer wake up …". Steve's fitting counter-question is, "What's different after this?" We are amazed that it can be so simple and so radical. The master goes one step further envisioning the miracle: "And if you (the client) have died, what is different? Who do you want to be at your funeral and who not, what should the ceremony be like?" And so on. We listen to him curiously, smiling and thoughtful. Will we have the courage to be so confrontationally solution-focused the next time? I often tell this story to my students during their training at ÖAS so that they can appreciate the two masters and their approach.

Back to my first day at the BFTC. The video cassette recorder suddenly stops working; therapy sessions are rescheduled so that Steve can go to get the recorder repaired straight away, because the functioning of the system has top priority. In one of the first articles published by the BFTC group (de Shazer et al., 1986), the video recording is identified as a core component in solution-oriented work. Eve Lipchik, who was a team member of this group, told me that, in the pioneering phase of the BFTC, the team spent a long time analysing the video tapes. Each step was discussed and all further steps were planned following the principle of maximum efficiency, and the following intervention was similarly recorded and the video checked. This is how the network of interventions slowly emerged, interventions which, much later, come together in the Central Map.

Suddenly the master looms in front of the mirror while Insoo continues the therapies without a break. Insoo is very resilient and tough. Unlike Steve, she is less willing to discuss issues, preferring to conduct therapies. She writes reluctantly. At that time she tells me that she is now planning her first book with a ghost-writer because writing is such an ordeal for her on account of her being bilingual. She wants to be interviewed, and then let the ghost-writer write the book (Berg, 1994). We know that she later wrote with others (for example Berg & Miller, 1992, De Jong and Berg, 1997).

Steve, on the other hand, enthuses about writing a thriller in his retirement. He is looking forward, for once in his life, to writing something really exciting. Regrettably, he died unexpectedly and did not achieve this goal.

What did I learn after the first day at BFTC?

That there is nothing mystical about solution-focused brief therapy; it proceeds in short, succinct steps; the impact on clients is monitored continuously; much is attempted and some efforts bear fruit; if something does not work, try doing it again differently – with patience and hard work you will be successful. The important thing is to never stop considering possible changes.

I learn that practice is simultaneously research into the concept of solution-focused brief therapy; the attitude behind the therapy hour is borne by the spirit of research. I learn that this form of therapy happens quickly, and that action, not interpretation, is to the fore; something must be done so that change is noticed and anchored.

I understand that meaning is relevant insofar as it contributes to a solution. Otherwise it is just noise that interferes with the positive melody on the way to the goal. Noises are ignored, the melody is underscored.

A Sunday in Milwaukee with Steve and Insoo

On Sunday Insoo is planning a barbecue for all students currently attending BFTC. Most are Asian and speak Insoo's language. Steve is to go shopping with me, so that we can have a barbecue in the afternoon. He seems a little vexed, but is willing. The traditional division of roles between the sexes, only the other way around: Steve goes shopping; Insoo shows a group of Asian students around the BFTC. Steve and I go to a Polish butcher in Milwaukee. Once there, he explains to me in glowing terms the different types of sausage. For him, they savour of a lost home – his beloved Polish-Jewish sausage roots. Steve asks me, perplexed, how many sausages we should buy. But I have no more idea than he how many people have said they will come. We buy in bulk, then wait in the garden for the Asian students who Insoo drove to BFTC for a "quick" visit. We assume that it won't take long, as it's Sunday, and so there can be no therapies. Steve asks me when we should start the barbeque, and of course I cannot answer this question any more than I could the previous one. Currently there are three of us: Steve, another northern European guest and myself. As a host: Steve is unsure, awkward; the woman of the house is missing. Sometime later we begin to cook, in the hope that the "others" will join us later. However, no one comes, and Insoo cannot be reached by phone. We have a relaxed and quiet meal, as we are not enough people to start up a discussion. In addition, we remain polite, restrained by the expectation of waiting for the others, or rather, of not having waited. The remaining meat slowly chars, a sad spectacle.

At half past nine Insoo arrives with the students; there was so much to do. No one is in a bad mood, despite the fact that there is nothing left to eat because the meat and sausages are just charred remains! There is always Kimchi (Korean pickled cabbage) and bread, either in the refrigerator or from Insoo's sister, who lives next door. The strong garlicky coal smell wafts through the house and garden. The Asians are happy and discuss eagerly and animatedly, so that, finally, our master is pleased.

"When students ask me if I work systemically, I first answer no", Steve says and then explains that the initial surprise is followed by an interesting discussion which becomes systemic. Much like the amusing dialogue which follows when the waiter takes your order and you ask for eight grains of rice, a truly ingenious communication. Steve recommends everyone in the group to give it a try. It is all about confusing the whole and its parts. Steve explains it with reference to Wittgenstein, but I cannot follow him. For myself, I imagine how confused a waiter might be if you ordered eight grains of rice. It probably makes a difference whether the waiter is an Asian or non-Asian waiter. He might think he is being made fun of. Yet the question, although strange, can be a creative question based on paradoxes – the showpieces of systemic methodology. The waiter might ask himself, "Why eight and not seven grains of rice?" And why it would be different if I had ordered eight sausages instead. He would have probably replied, "with mustard, ketchup, and with or without fries?" And is this a different question from the one earlier today about the number of sausages for our afternoon barbecue? Are closeness to practical everyday life and playfulness with words related? Is this about practical things or just thoughts? And once again, an idea occurs to me; it's about the ingenious combination of practicality and intellect. Let me recapitulate. Solution Focused Brief Therapy is not at all easy! The parts and the whole in the preconception of language, the play with words, embedded in visible deeds, that aspect of ever-present evaluation, and a hint of the "American way of life".

Steve now arrives at his punch line concerning Gregory Bateson. When students indicated that they had finally understood him, he asked himself what he had done wrong..., ha, ha, ha. For my part, I experience Steve de Shazer very similarly to his description of the master Gregory Bateson. His remarks are deliberately confusing, and so we struggle to understand. We are actively trying to decipher what is being concealed, that is, we think! The conversations are slightly paradoxical, ambiguous, funny and sometimes only obliquely accessible...which probably explains its closeness to jazz music, which Steve emphasises again and again. And we know, of course, that Steve was himself a jazz musician.

The resemblance of Steve's approach to paradoxical interventions explains the rapport that later arose between Steve de Shazer and Insoo Kim Berg and the constellation work of Matthias Varga von Kibéd and Insa Sparrer at SySt, the masters of the paradox in German-speaking countries.

During the two weeks in Milwaukee at BFTC I get a hint of the imaginative richness and creativity which later enables me to read Steve's books differently and to understand the touch of irony, wit and paradoxical humour that allows the solution-oriented approach to appear simultaneously playful and logical; I can sense genius. Unlike Insoo, who explains her techniques practically and pragmatically and with great didactic skill so that she is a joy to watch, Steve is the artist who considers the intricacies and logical loops, who follows the production of a "work" intellectually. Insoo is constantly working, empathetic, thoughtful, approaching people. Her therapy sessions are elegant, beautiful and exciting all at once, while with Steve one often has the impression that his words disappear into nothingness. Nevertheless, his clients often laugh – with him. Maybe the humour is just too strange for a European woman like me. In Vienna, I then read his first books in English – "Keys to Solution" and later "Clues". I would have understood many things differently or not at all, had I not been there previously. The solution-focused virus has infected me! And I am extremely happy because it is a lot of fun to think and to work in this manner. It's so fresh, unencumbered, progressive.

As a trainer I observe later repeatedly how my students like to use the solution-oriented approach as a compendium of recipes. Learned quickly, you want to apply it successfully. Complicated aspects like paradoxes, the constant reformulations and focus on the idea for a solution are difficult and require a lot of patience. Even the masters in their books want to keep it simple, "easy for the learner", but this has allowed misunderstandings to arise which have been harmful for brief therapeutic work. It all sounds so easy, so simple. I explain to our students that the solution-oriented approach is the result of a brilliant collaboration between client and therapist, where every sentence is precisely crafted and new formulations are continuously created and tested. Every intervention must fit exactly and the timing of the delivery must be carefully considered. Success results from repetition and from the creative efforts of those therapists who can play with the right words. It is not really a technique; it is art, music-making.

Some students get into the swing of it and start to read the master's books, while others cling on to the recipes. This latter decision often leads to misunderstandings regarding the solution-oriented model.

Insoo and Steve in Vienna

As I receive the two of them in Vienna for the first time, I want to be their tour guide, to show them all the sights and attractions of our city. But the two have other plans, because in each new city they do exactly the same: toss a coin to determine which direction the city tour will take, heads for left, tails for right. At each corner they come to, let the coin decide in which direction they should go. Thus they come without any preconceptions to places that have been selected by chance. They discover the city in their own way. When they are tired, they just take a taxi back to the hotel. I remain frustrated at home and learn the next day all the places they visited. I can't help feeling that the places they describe are uninteresting and irrelevant. I'm almost offended that they don't apprehend my city as I would wish as their host. Why were they not at St. Stephen's Cathedral, Karlsplatz or in Vienna's city centre? I wanted them to be excited about Vienna and enjoy its flair.

Thank God I remember the time we spent together in Milwaukee; Steve and Insoo are just different. They live their lives under the constant prompting of coincidences. Coping with randomness enables one to expect arbitrary decisions, thereby improving the possibility for change. This alternation between chance and arbitrariness is an essential part of the solution-oriented approach and its inventors live by it. As their hostess, I learn suddenly what it means to surrender to chance, what one gives up and what one obtains. The next day I listen attentively to their descriptions of places and buildings in Vienna, which were unknown to me until now. Since I have come to love and accept my masters now, I can translate their approach to their way of doing therapy; it is rethinking which is the prerequisite for good ideas, not spontaneous notions or good-sounding words. And only so can the cooperation between client and therapist arise.

The discussion of the first Viennese solution-oriented team with the masters

After a year of therapy with a team at the Institute for Marriage and Family Therapy, which works exclusively according to the solution-oriented model, some clients take their leave as follows: "It was a good time, but you have this method, eh, where there is a lot of praise, that's your way of luring us ... so that we try hard to do something!" Some Viennese clients have survived our purist style of intervention with no scars. The typical client at the Praterstrasse was the one who at Eve Lipchik's Live Supervision sensed that a quick end was intended and then went on to remain at the Institute for many years! We discussed this at the next workshop with Steve; after all, Vienna is the birthplace of psychoanalysis and this is significant, because in Vienna people like to grumble, complain, harp on about their woes … such is the golden Viennese soul … and we must allow room for this when treating the local clients. In five minutes we manage to list twenty words in the Viennese dialect for "complain". Steve is impressed and acknowledges the cultural relevance of our enumeration. Nevertheless, he does not see why therapy should therefore last longer. We counter: if we praise too early, our clients feel they are not being taken seriously.

I myself have remained loyal to this understanding of solution focused therapy, which does not hold the view that shorter is better, but which offers solutions individually tailored to the tempo and therapeutic relationship. I've always had good experiences when I allow the client to rant, as long as I do not let them hypnotise me and I choose the right moment to advance to the solution. I believe that when solution-oriented therapy progresses too rapidly it has an alienating effect, at least in some parts of Europe, although this cultural nuance has no significant effect on the use of the instrument as such. Eve Lipchik has written several articles and a book (Lipchik, 2011) on the subject of speed and solution.

Today, I personally do not doubt that I am practising solution-focused therapy, even if this may not seem so judged by the number of sessions. Ultimately, it does not matter for me whether I include the past from the client's biography, if I can make good use of the story for future solutions. From the perspective of a desired future, I can use my client's past as a resource, as an exception or as contradiction. The sloppy radical verbal battles of our masters on topics such as task, objective and solution have given way to the therapist's everyday experience. Through the active use of the model, irrespective of whatever conditions may prevail in therapeutic practice, its universal usefulness is proven once again and it remains true to itself.

References

Berg, I. K. (1994). *Family Based Services: A Solution-Based Approach.* New York: Norton.

Berg, I. K. and Miller, S. D. (1992). *Working with the Problem Drinker: A Solution-Focused Approach.* New York: Norton.

De Jong, P. & Berg, I. K. (1997). *Interviewing for Solutions.* Belmont CA: Wadsworth.

de Shazer, S. (1985). *Keys to Solution in Brief Therapy.* New York: Norton.

de Shazer, S. (1988). *Clues: Investigating Solutions in Brief Therapy.* New York: Norton.

de Shazer, S., Berg, I. K., Lipchik, E., Nunnally, E., Molnar, A., Wallace, G., & Weiner-Davis, M. (1986). Brief therapy – Targeted development of solutions. *Family Dynamics 11*, 182–205.

Lipchik, E. (2011). *On the need to wear two hats.* Heidelberg: Carl Auer Verlag GmbH.

Corinna Ahlers is a psychologist, systemic family therapist and trainer for systemic family therapy in Vienna (Austrian Society for Systemic Therapy and Systemic Studies – ÖAS), for the Institute for Marriage and Family Therapy of Vienna, currently in private practice, specialising in separation, patchwork, and continued families.

Marianne and Kaspar Baeschlin   Winterthur, Switzerland

Steve de Shazer and educators

In 1980, in a large old farmhouse in Winterthur, Switzerland, we founded the Grundhof Werkschule, a residential special education facility for young men who could no longer be accommodated in the elementary school system. Until 2000, we lived together on this farm with nine young people and our own three children. In addition to the academic classes, we managed the farm, its animals and garden together with the adolescents. We treated everything we did as school experience. It served the learning and development of these young people who had a lot of catching up to do.

Our employees were trained special education and social workers. We were idealistic, committed teachers. In the first 10 years we gave our best for these neglected children, and we wanted to get to the root of the problems; we wanted to understand and, armed with this knowledge, solve the problems. All of our team meetings and case conferences were problem-oriented; we took on a lot of responsibility, which was a burden. The behavioural problems of the young people were sometimes excessive and after those first 10 years, we were exhausted and close to giving up.

In spring 1992, we happened to meet Steve de Shazer in Heidelberg. For us that was a decisive experience: this man standing at the front on the podium, saying, *"You don't have to know the problem to find the solution"*. After all those years, trying to recognise and resolve the problems of our students, this remark seemed like a joke – and yet at the same time it fascinated us. Intuitively, we felt that this new way of thinking meant salvation for us and our work. We began to change our thinking and to see things in a new way.

At that time residential care was authoritarian. The development processes for the children were conceived and controlled by psycholo-

gist sitting in their ivory tower. The teacher merely had the dreary task
of providing the framework and discipline.

However, there were already signs of revised thinking, for example,
in a book entitled *The Other 23 Hours* (Trieschman, Whittaker and
Brendtro, 1969). One hour of therapy per day, yes. But what happens
with the kids in the remaining 23 hours? That was the issue for us. We
wanted to modernise the educational effort, and thereby add value and
make it more attractive. But soon we realised that the entire solution-
oriented literature at the time was written for therapeutic settings. All
solution-oriented discussions were conceived as therapy sessions.

We were immediately convinced that this approach would be
perfectly suited to pedagogical work. How our world changed as we
started to discuss with the students what they could do, instead of what
they could not do, and what we wanted from them rather than what we
did not want. This shift of focus fundamentally changed our lives as
educators.

Inspired by the solution-oriented approach and somewhat naively,
we signed up straight away for the four-week training in Milwaukee. In
the summer of 1993 we were able to participate. Mathias Wehrli and
Kaspar Baeschlin, the two Grundhof teachers, travelled to Milwaukee.
Besides us two schoolteachers from Switzerland, the course was only
attended by therapists.

Steve was quite confused when he heard of our profession. He kept
saying that he had nothing to do with the school system, and talked
about his own bad experiences with teachers who always knew better
and insisted stubbornly that he understood nothing of pedagogy. He
called us "the two odd fellows". He could not imagine what we wanted
to get out of the course, because the most important task in the training
was the therapeutic conversation with real clients and the subsequent
evaluation.

Insoo had a better feeling for the issues which interested us professionally, since she had already coached and advised employees at the
Milwaukee social security office. Our final task at the end of the training
was to give some thought to implementing the solution-oriented
approach in a special school. Insoo was extremely helpful here. She

assisted us in developing a new concept and, more and more, Steve warmed to our questions.

In the following years, we introduced the solution-oriented approach in the Grundhof School and, parallel to this, in other social pedagogical institutions. We found out what tools were useful and what was not suitable. Primarily it was Insoo, but then over time increasingly Steve, who was interested in this process and supported us in transferring the therapeutic approach to the field of education.

For 10 years, from 1994 to 2004, we organised two workshops per year for educators and teachers. Steve came for three days in the spring, Insoo for three days during autumn. In these workshops, we worked primarily on educational issues, such as the sense and nonsense of penalties or how rules and frameworks could be turned into resources. Steve still abided by his original statement that he understood nothing of pedagogy. He said, *"I do not do kids"*. However, when he met our students, he was quite different. His love and respect for these people, who had to live in difficult situations, was evident. He had his own special way "to do kids". On one occasion, all the students sat with us and Steve at the round table, posing all manner of possible and impossible questions to the famous man from America. He willingly and patiently answered every question, whereas the questions of workshop participants often left Steve shaking his head, annoyed by the clever talk.

In support discussions with our young students, Steve was all ears and consistently asked what they wanted, put scaling questions to them and gave brief, but very appropriate feedback. He provoked us all to think and reflect. From Steve we learned always to follow the client, to take an interest in what he says and ask about what works. We learned to refrain from commentaries, following Steve's sentiment: "I do not read between the lines because there is nothing there".

Insoo brought her spontaneity, her kindness. In conversations with our young people her loud "wow" was an expression of appreciation that erupted again and again. Her youthful gaiety and light-heartedness created an atmosphere of respect and confidence. Once, when she went for a walk after lunch and was a little late for the afternoon workshop, a student picked her up on his moped. Reclining on the luggage rack, she was chauffeured back, laughing and full of life.

We are very grateful that we met Steve and Insoo and, with their support, were able to assist in anchoring the solution-oriented attitude in education.

Reference

Trieschman, A. E., Whittaker, J. K. & Brendtro, L. K. (1969). The Other 23 Hours: Child Care Work with Emotionally Disturbed Children in a Therapeutic Milieu,. Piscataway NJ: Transaction Publishers.

Marianne and Kaspar Baeschlin are special education teachers in Winterthur, Switzerland. They are founders and directors of the Grundhof School and of the Centre for Solution-Focused Consultation.

Janet Beavin Bavelas   Victoria, BC, Canada

Memories of Steve and Insoo

In the early 1990s, several local therapists were organising workshops that brought leading therapists here to Vancouver Island. Two of the organisers were my graduate students, who thought it would be a great idea to add an extra "research day" at the University, where the visitors could learn about our team's current projects. I cannot say that these meetings were usually a success. Most visitors did not see the relevance of presumably "positivist" lab research with undergraduate psychology students and appeared to be politely bored. Insoo and Steve were the dramatic exception. From their first visit in 1995, they understood completely and enthusiastically that research on dialogue was relevant to SFBT. Our affinity for each other's work was immediate and only grew stronger. Insoo began to send us their videos as soon as these were published, and students such as Bruce Phillips (1998, 1999), Dan McGee (1999, 2005), and Christine Tomori (2004, 2007) quickly chose to analyse these, rather than experimental data, for their thesis projects. (See these and later publications at   http://web.uvic.ca/psyc/bavelas /CommunPsychother.php) And Steve and Insoo started inviting me to speak at SFBT meetings.

Although 1995 was our first formal meeting, Insoo, Steve, and I probably met earlier, at least in passing, at the Mental Research Institute in Palo Alto. (I worked with the Palo Alto Group from 1961 to 1970 and still visited the Brief Therapy Center after I moved to Canada.) Certainly the time that Steve, Insoo, and I each spent there was formative, especially because of John Weakland, who was an important mentor to all three of us. Going back even further, I think that what attracted each of us to the Palo Alto Group in the first place, and espe-cially to John, were some characteristics (or quirks!) that we had in common: (i) a profound interest in language and how it actually functions in conversations; (ii) an attraction to any good idea that is 180° from the currently unquestioned ideas; (iii) an ethical commitment to treating people respectfully, both in person and in assumptions or theories about them; and (iv) a preference for collaboration rather than individual achievement. This unusual configuration of common passions and values easily spanned the distance between therapy and experimental psychology (cf. Bavelas, 2011).

My time with Insoo and Steve was shorter than most of those who write their memories here, and it was sporadic rather than continuous, necessarily fitted around my academic life. Sometimes the two worlds came together, such as when Steve was appointed the Dean's External Examiner (the person with the final word) for Dan McGee's 1999 doctoral oral. I'm sure Steve found that role ironic, given his own experience in (and opinion of) graduate school.

My last conversations with Steve were emails about the possibility of designing an experiment on the essentials of Miracle Questioning. As few other therapists do, he understood the necessity to translate abstractions into specific procedures with the hard thinking that is also the rewarding core of experimentation. After he died, I was very surprised when Insoo asked me to deliver the opening tribute to Steve at a 2006 conference in Amsterdam. I hesitated because I'm not a therapist, but agreed – with trepidation. After several unsatisfactory versions about therapy, I finally followed the advice often given to writers: Write what you know about. So I presented what I knew about, which is microanalysis research on the details of dialogue. The tribute became video excerpts of Steve's therapeutic brilliance as revealed in tiny, moment-by-moment details of his interviews, such as the eloquent variety of his *m-hm's*. The reaction to this presentation showed me the legacy that Steve and Insoo's teaching had created—everyone got it! They recognised this research method as if they had known it all along, and they understood its relevance for SFBT, just as Steve and Insoo had done 10 years earlier.

The last time I saw Insoo in person was our informal conversation, together with Peter De Jong and Harry Korman, after the November 2006 SFBTA meeting in Denver. We were talking entirely about research, about the need to keep publicising the evidence base but also to add new dimensions to it. Once again, Insoo said she wanted to learn about microanalysis. So I challenged her to finally make time to come to Victoria and learn it. Peter and Harry were also interested, and all of us committed to meet in Victoria the third week of August the following year. Being Insoo, she soon expanded it to more people and moved the plan to Milwaukee. Before we had time to work out the details, she died. But Jennifer Gerwing, Sara Healing, Christine Tomori and I hosted 10 solution-focused colleagues in Victoria that week in August. It was our first microanalysis workshop and has generated almost 20 more, large and small, to date. It also led to over a dozen completed or continuing research projects with SFBT colleagues. The merger of SFBT with a new kind of research and training is well underway, a continuing tribute to Steve and Insoo.

Post Script

During the 1996 Therapeutic Conversations three meeting that Insoo and Steve had arranged for me to speak at, Steve spontaneously asked me to sit in on his discussion panel. It was about therapy topics, so I hung back and let the others respond to the questions from the audience. However, there was one question about dealing with grief for a dead friend or relative, especially the continuing reminders of all the new things in one's life that this person will never know about or share with you.

Surprising myself, I spoke up and questioned whether we had to think of this sharing as absolutely lost. My position is not spiritual or supernatural; it's just part of the social beings that we are. Think of the living friends and relatives whom you know very well, including how they would react in certain situations. So, even when you don't see them very often, it's possible to imagine how amused, annoyed, intrigued, etc., one of them would be at something you're doing or thinking. You may never even tell that person subsequently, but you have fully imagined sharing a moment with him or her. My point is that we carry these important people in our heads, as well as in our hearts. This connection doesn't disappear when they die, because they live on in our knowledge of them. We can still enjoy how they *would have* reacted.

Steve's panel discussion went on to other topics and was finally over. As we were leaving the platform, he leaned over and said with some pleasure, "Yeah. I still have great arguments with John" (Weakland, who had died the previous year). I'm happy to say that I sometimes imagine Steve's or Insoo's reactions to things that would be interesting, annoying, or delightful to us. I hope that you who are reading this book have some of these shared moments as well.

Reference

Bavelas, J. (2011). Connecting the lab to the therapy room. Microanalysis, co-construction, and Solution-focused therapy. In C. Franklin, T. Trepper, W. J. Gingerich, and E. McCollum (Eds.) *Solution-focused Brief Therapy: A handbook of evidence-based practice* (pp. 144–162). Oxford: Oxford University Press.

Janet Beavin Bavelas Ph.D, FRSC is Professor Emeritus of Psychology, University of Victoria, British Columbia, Canada. She is a consultant and lecturer in the Department of Psychology.

Hans Benniks   Hilversum, Netherlands

How Steve de Shazer influenced my life as a therapist

I met Steve de Shazer for the first time on the Korzybski Institute Mastercourse in Bruges in the autumn of 2003. On the day Steve had given his presentation, I was invited by Luc Isebaert to a joint dinner at Luc's house in de Haan, a beautiful village situated at the Belgian coast not far from Bruges.

What struck me during dinner was that Steve talked about Milton Erickson and his work. At that time I was and still am now very interested in the work of Erickson and particularly in its practical application. I had noticed when I was reading solution-oriented literature and books that little or no reference was made by the authors to Erickson and his work. That is why I was so pleasantly surprised by Steve de Shazer.

Besides the parts of Erickson's work I did understand, there were parts which I didn't understand at all, even after reading and re-reading. I was glad to discover I was not the only one, I understood that Steve and his team had studied it deeply.

Steve came up against a growing number of Erickson's case descriptions which, although very successful, also remained totally incomprehensible. What theory and intervention underpinned it remained a mystery. And worse ... the 'incomprehensible' stack was getting bigger. Steve turned the cases around and around and upside down, did everything to understand it better, but it remained unclear (de Shazer, 1988, 1994). It seemed that Milton Erickson found no need for a psychological theory. Rather, if questions were asked he came up with an answer in the form of a case description, a story, an anecdote or a metaphor.

However, this did not make understanding his way of working any clearer.

In the solution-oriented model by Steve de Shazer and his team there are many Ericksonian techniques and indirect suggestions, such as the yes-set, the miracle question (pseudo-orientation in the time/crystal ball technique of Erickson), the session break, compliments and utilisation. At one of the Erickson conferences in Arizona Steve said, "There is no day passing where I don't use something from him".

Steve saw the session break during the treatment as a trance-induction, because the client, by waiting, becomes more receptive to what the therapist is going to say when he or she returns. Also the client is more open for compliments and the strengthening of the exceptions which have been discovered. Steve saw hypnotic behaviour at this point, such as changes in breathing, non-verbal behaviour and increasing relaxation. It also means that tasks can be accepted more easily.

Erickson's utilisation principle is to take advantage of everything you are offered by the client, such as behaviour, thoughts, resistance and feelings. Steve supplemented this with the idea of using everything that is accurate, meaningful, effective or good.

After a lot of effort in the search for the essence of Erickson's work, Steve de Shazer found out that Erickson asked his clients about their thoughts concerning what would be the best solution and this was utilised in the treatment. Steve discovered that his focus on therapy was wrongly addressed; the client is most important, not the therapist. The most unusual interventions came from the client themselves.

One of my favourite techniques is to ask scaling questions – in particular, where the therapist asks the client about the reactions of the environment, such as the partner, friends and parents. What strikes me here is that the figures which the client thinks that the others would give are often higher than the client would give themselves.

Giving indirect suggestions in a general sense is also a favourite idea. Naturally this must of course be connected to the treatment, the purpose and the type of client. For me as a therapist, the most attractive aspect of the form of therapy developed by Steve is having structure that can be used not as binding protocol but as a flexible directive. In that way, it can still connect with the client and their wishes, to factors in the client's life; it gives hope to the client and connects to the resilience of the client.

In conclusion, Steve de Shazer has had a lot of influence on my way of working and thinking; and through Steve the work of Erickson also became clearer. Steve found out, after initially giving up his attempts, that he had studied the wrong person – namely Erickson the great therapist – instead of the client. Erickson often asked his clients how they thought about change(s). In other words, Erickson asked the client to provide his own ideas that could lead to the best solution and utilised it. The most unusual interventions came from the client themselves.

Outcome research in psychotherapy confirms this vision: utilise, and make use of the feedback you get from your client! Steve de Shazer and Milton H. Erickson are still for me the most important 'living' resources.

References

de Shazer, S. (1988). Utilization: The Foundation of Solutions. In J. K. Zeig & S. R. Lankton (Eds.), *Developing Ericksonian Therapy: A State of the Art* (pp. 112–126). New York: Brunner/Mazel.

de Shazer, S. (1994). Essential, Non-Essential: Vive la Différence. In J. K. Zeig (Ed.), *Ericksonian Methods, The Essence of the Story* (pp. 240–252). New York: Brunner/Mazel.

Hans L. Benniks is a practising psychologist in Hilversum, the Netherlands. He is a teacher at Rino Noord Holland, SPON, Radboud University Nijmegen, President of the Milton Erickson Institute Netherlands and former Board Member of EBTA.

Ursula Bühlmann-Stahli   Bern, Switzerland

Encounters for life

In 1993 I came as an inexperienced senior physician to the paediatric and adolescent psychiatric service in Biel, Switzerland. Until then, I had gained experience mainly in paediatrics, and knew little about psychiatry. The colleagues at the institution gave me a warm and generous welcome. They had already looked into and worked with the solution-and resource-oriented approach of Steve de Shazer and Insoo Kim Berg. I was also taken with this approach: as a newcomer to the paediatric and adolescent psychiatry scene, I was glad to have practical and useful tools for my work. In 1998 a colleague asked me whether we might undertake an advanced, in-depth training in solution-oriented therapy. The Milton-Erickson Institute at Heidelberg (Gunther Schmidt) had announced a series of three advanced training sessions with Steve, each lasting three days. I decided to sign up on the spot. And so we embarked on our first meeting with Steve.

Even the train ride from Bern to Heidelberg was an experience; we had to change three times each way and were always curious as to what would be waiting for us next. The first time we planned our trip poorly, arriving a few minutes late. We tried to explain and to apologise. Steve just said, "If you are not two minutes early, you are too late", a principle he learned from his grandfather. Later, my own children (now 16 and 18) got to hear this from me when they came too late (and were no doubt irritated now and then). And in this way the children and my husband occasionally encountered Steve.

The days in Heidelberg with Steve fascinated me from the start. He often spoke from the heart; what I learned from him fitted very well with my own beliefs and ideas. He astonished us all continually, for example, when confronted with the question, "Why do you ask the miracle question at just this juncture?" he replied tersely, "Why not?" Or to the question, "What do you do if the client has a relapse?" Steve replied, "There is no relapse". At times we would have appreciated more detailed explanations. Nevertheless, we somehow understood what he meant.

Then, the second part of the training: Steve had told us to bring videos of our work. I summoned up all my courage and volunteered when he asked who wanted to show their video. As I said, I was still inexperienced. I remember that the video contained a sequence with a family who had already undertaken therapies with other therapists. I know that I was really toiling in the video sequence, suggesting many ideas for solutions and doing whatever else one does when one is a little clueless. Suddenly Steve pressed the pause button on the video cassette recorder and said that if he had been sitting behind the one-way mirror, he would have called out to me in the meeting room, **Ursula, you are working too hard**. I understood. This one sentence of his has accompanied and helped me now for so many years. It comes to me when I realise that I am once again trying too hard, when I want to achieve the solution for the client, when my impatience causes me to move one step ahead instead of "leading from one step behind" as Steve always said. This sentence echoes in the ears of my intervision colleagues again and again, and I have certainly recounted it in supervisions and elsewhere. And thus many of my colleagues encounter Steve without having met him directly.

I also fondly remember the evenings after the course in "The Rose" restaurant in Heidelberg where we went for supper. Steve liked to order a pork chop and a beer (note: my mother is from Bavaria, so I appreciated his choice.) Steve also sometimes appeared reserved in this setting, even taciturn. But I was fascinated by his completely open manner of tackling things without prejudice; this way of thinking without "pigeonholing" or jumping to conclusions. I felt connected to him, in some indescribable way even though we did not speak much with each other.

During those days in Heidelberg I learned much. I was able to apply what I had heard immediately in my everyday therapeutic work. The ideas of the solution- and resource-focused approach, and especially those days with Steve in Heidelberg, have heavily influenced me; I am an avowed fan. The approach helps me to have fun while working, an important factor for my mental health. Throughout my professional career, Steve accompanied me; he was present and continues to be so. How did he manage this, to be present for so many people over the years? And this, although some only met him briefly, and others not at all?

I am very glad that I was later able to attend a workshop with Insoo in Bern. I liked her fresh, lively manner. I had seen Insoo many times on video. But to experience her live was something else. Her manner was infectious, and I found her work fascinating.

With Insoo and Steve I had the feeling that they always asked the right question at the right time. To this day, I sometimes ask myself during conversations with clients what Steve or Insoo would now ask them. How would they cope with situations and obstacles? This gives me new ideas, or other points of view, and I often let Steve's suggestions inspire me. "If it works, do more of it. If it doesn't, try something else".

Thus Steve and Insoo are always present in my life, in my work as a psychotherapist, but sometimes also in my role as a mother and wife, daughter and friend, and all the other guises I adopt along the way.

I am very grateful that I was able to meet Steve and Insoo. And I am glad to be able to say, once again here, **THANK YOU.**

Ursula Bühlmann-Stahli MD is a specialist in paediatric and adolescent psychiatry and psychotherapy; FMH in private practice in Bern, Switzerland, and Board member of the Network for solution-oriented work, Switzerland.

Hélène Dellucci   Lyon, France

My encounter with Steve de Shazer and Insoo Kim Berg

Meeting Steve

Like many solutionists, I met solution focused therapy like a "journey home" to values, an attitude I already adhered to, and of which I tried to convince first my professors, then my colleagues, and later my students. It wasn't necessary to convince the people who came seeking for help. They shared it straightaway.

By meeting Pascal Soubeyrand I learned, through the Bruges model (Isebaert & Cabié, 1997), how important choice is and that people always have very good and constructive reasons to do what they do.

I often heard Luc Isebaert telling the stories of his first meetings with Steve in the early eighties.

"Could it be that simple?!"

Even though I was not there at that moment, through Luc's voice I can see Steve de Shazer puzzled, considering the scope of solution focused implications through this statement. Today, it still resonates in my ears when I see people reprocess trauma, connecting resources, and making a "good learning experience" out of it. I would like to have had the opportunity to talk about trauma reprocessing with Steve and Insoo. I am sure that, even though not agreeing about the usefulness of emotions in therapy (I learned from Eve Lipchick that Steve and Insoo weren't interested in emotions), Steve could have raised his eyebrows at the simplicity of solution focused EMDR.

"Could it be that simple ?!" There seems still much to discover about the implications of this statement.

In psychotraumatology we say that if people are still alive, then they have found a way to survive, whatever happened to them. The longer the list of traumas, the stronger the list of the surviving resources. It is the therapist's job to help people to raise awareness about those specially developed skills from implicit memory to conscience. Close to Maturana & Varela's (1973) constructivist perspective[1], about the usefulness of the distinction between therapist's and client's expertise and knowledge, Steve taught us that we don't even need to know about the content of the client's stories. Our aim as therapists is to know more about the client's "resource structure", and make him/her/them more aware of it.

I really only met Steve once, at the EBTA conference in Amsterdam (2004) and I didn't know that this would be the first but also the last time I saw him in person. But I have the feeling that I met Steve many times through the vivid accounts of Luc Isebaert, Yvonne Dolan, Alasdair Macdonald and Ferdinand Wolf, which I was eager to listen to.

"Using the body as a resource in trauma therapy" would not have been easy to discuss at first sight with him, but I would have been proud to tell Steve that in my mind solution focused values are what works the best with trauma survivors, even though therapy with them, although safe enough, is often not brief.

---

[1] Through their Autopoïesis Theory, Maturana and Varela had discovered two basic conditions out of their question, "What makes a cell be alive and stay alive?" First, there must be a border, a membrane which makes the inner content of the cell distinct from the outside environment and, second, one cell must be distinct from the neighbouring cells. Both rules have been implemented as the basic condition for a family to be a family (Neuburger, 1995). Especially with trauma survivors, who more than others have experienced that their integrity has not been safe in the past, those rules are relevant in present interventions. Solution focused values, by basically making a distinction between the expertise of the therapist and the people seeking help, follow those rules strongly.

Meeting Insoo

When I think about how Steve said, "Everything I know, I stole from Insoo", it becomes obvious how much Insoo Kim Berg had the solution focused values embodied in her way of being with others, when acting therapeutically. In trauma therapy we state as a process rule, "Don't let go, until a soothing compromise has been found, while being flexible". That's completely what Insoo did: she stuck strongly and obsessively to the slightest sign so that she could fit in solution focused perspective, even in the worst stories people could tell.

This basic attitude becomes clear through Insoo's basic assumptions about children and parents (Berg & Steiner, 2003). Having these ideas in mind gives the therapist glasses of hope to look through. In social psychology, Snyder (1984) and colleagues (Snyder & Stukas, 1999) have shown, through research into social influence and stereotypes, how important the lens of perception is in shaping realities. I use this research as the main argument in solution focused teaching when it comes to the question, "Why solution focused?" Minimal research in established disciplines has always been very convincing.

When Insoo states kindly in a school class (Berg & Huibers, 2007), "I will write down everything you do well", no one really understands how serious she is about this. Deeply rooted in our Judeo-Christian education, where bad behaviour is the sin to eradicate, it is so easy to be irritated when children escape the adult's "well-meaning" control. What a surprise, when Insoo, at the end of the class, explains very concretely, by using her body, what she observed in the children's behaviour. By doing this, she raises awareness about behaviour which is normally not even noticed. And while she is doing this, she leaves out dramatically what makes the main focus in irritated teachers. Everybody seems to discover a new reality. Ferdinand Wolf and myself have extended those basic assumptions – Ferdinand by focusing on networking and professionals, and me for so-called "difficult clients" (Dellucci & Wolf, 2011). "Difficult clients" become difficult because the therapist begins to suffer, doesn't know what to do, and adopts, one by one, negative assumptions about the person he/she is trying to help. Trauma survivors in particular, who still behave as if they are in survival mode, can have this effect on good and willing helpers. They are not difficult, they are just different, by first and throughout testing the therapist's capacity to really respect their integrity, even at the most archaic level of functioning.

Insoo, by her way of being, invited therapists to engage in this sensorimotor dimension. This made her interventions integrated from movement, through explicitly shown surprise and other emotion, up to the cognitive level where she didn't deviate in the slightest from her strongly-held basic assumptions. We know today that through the mirroring neurobiology of our brains, we can influence each other by what we feel physiologically, emotionally and what we think. So staying hopeful, calm and centred by deciding what we look at shapes the reality in the therapy room very differently.

I also met Insoo just once in person, at the same moment I met Steve. They both disappeared too early, with the part of them of which we have to renounce. But at the same time, another part of them stays alive, through the myriad of memories, discussions and teachings, sprinkled with anecdotes which leave the listener with a vivd sense of shared experience, because the solution focused community still continues what Steve and Insoo initiated.

My deep gratitude goes also to my teachers, colleagues and all those who shared these vivid memories and made it possible for me to connect through my special way of implementing solution focused approach in EMDR and the healing work with complex trauma survivors and their families.

References

Berg, I. K. & Steiner, T. (2003). *Children's solution work*. New York: Norton.

Berg, I. K. & Huibers, A. (2007). *Classroom solutions*. DVD. Solutions Center, Utrecht, The Netherlands.

Dellucci, H. & Wolf, F. (2011). Choisir ses représentations service de plus de confort et d'efficacité dans la relation d'aide. *Thérapie Familiale*, 32(2), 275–291.

Isebaert, L. & Cabié, M.-C. (1997). *Pour une thérapie brève. Le libre choix du patient comme éthique en psychothérapie,* Ramonville Saint-Agne: Ed Erès.

Maturana, H. R. & Varela, F. J. (1973 for the 1st edition), (1980). Autopoïesis and Cognition : the Realization of the Living. In R. S. Cohen & M. W. Wartofsky (Eds.), Boston Studies in the Philosophy of Science 42. Dordrecht : D. Reidel Publishing Co.

Neuburger, R. (1995). *Le mythe familial.* Paris: ESF.

Snyder, M. (1984). When belief creates reality. *Advances in Experimental Social Psychology, 18,* 250.

Snyder, M. & Stukas, A. A. (1999). Interpersonal Process : the interplay of cognitive, motivational and behavioral activities in social interaction. *Annual Review of Psychology, 50,* 273–303.

Hélène Dellucci is a psychologist, systemic family therapist and EMDR consultant in private practice in Lyon, France. She is active as a supervisor and trainer. Main topics: solution-focused and body-oriented trauma therapy for patients with dissociative illness.

Kirsten Dierolf   Frankfurt, Germany

Found in translation

In 2001, I was mainly doing Inner Game trainings and coachings for managers as part of a small consultancy in Freiburg. I was interested in attending a post-conference workshop with Timothy Gallwey, the founder of Inner Game, at the 2001 coaching conference in Grindelwald. Luckily, the organiser of the pre and post conference workshops, Peter Szabó, agreed to have me translate another workshop and swap the fee for Gallwey's. My first degrees were in theology and linguistics and I had taken the exam as a certified translator for English, but I did not have a lot of experience in simultaneous translation. Therefore, the preparation consisted of listening to the workshop leader's tapes.

What I heard on the tape was a friendly (and luckily slow) Asian-English voice and a content that wowed me to the point that I forgot that what I really wanted to do was prepare for the translation. The people I was to translate for three days were Insoo Kim Berg and Louis Cauffman. Why was I so wowed even by just listening to the "A tap on the shoulder" tape and by reading *Interviewing for Solutions* (De Jong & Berg, 1997)?

I had always been interested in all things "mind" and also very interested in helping people lead the kind of lives they want to lead. Yet, at this time, all attempts to pursue this interest had been thwarted by the weird ways people usually went about this endeavour. I had tried pastoral counselling and was told I would have to examine my own family history before being able to help anyone (this did not follow at all for me), so I did not enroll in that class. All my fellow students who did enroll became very odd – interpreting people's behaviour in very strange and disrespectful ways. I still remember someone running away from a philosophical argument that I was winning with the words, "You have such father issues!" So, I had given up trying to be helpful to others and had downgraded my interest in all things mind to a curious pastime, and engaged in it only by reading philosophy and linguistic texts with a passion.

You can imagine how things started to click when I translated for Insoo and Louis. Here was an approach that was looking at the surface of helping people and also gelled really well with what I had learned about post-structural linguistics and philosophy of mind (not that I was conscious of this at the time, but this is how I now explain the "click"). Somehow I did not seem to have botched up the translation too much and was therefore invited to translate for Insoo and also for Steve, both at Peter Szabó and Daniel Meier's coaching school and at other places in Switzerland and Germany.

Most of what I know about Solution Focus started as small insights during these translations. The first time I had to translate a Solution Focused interview with a live client in Winterthur, for example, I translated consecutively, like I had been taught. The client spoke, I took notes, and when she had finished, I translated for Steve. He did not like that … actually, it didn't work well at all. The client kept talking about her problem (which at this point I thought was really normal and the way a therapy session should work) and since he didn't understand, Steve couldn't interrupt or react in any way. It later dawned on me that an SF session is truly based on therapist and client "doing something together", co-creating the conversation.

The more traditional model of communication, sender-receiver (or in our case sender- translator- receiver), wasn't appropriate here and did not work. So I started translating sentence for sentence, realising how Steve was picking up certain words and not others, trying to reproduce what he was doing in English in German and what the client was doing in German in English. It was very challenging, but reminiscing now, I realise how wonderful this opportunity was.

I also translated for Insoo and Steve during workshops. Sometimes people would ask questions of the form, "Does Solution Focus work with *insert favourite diagnosis*?" I would dutifully translate into English and Steve would simply look puzzled and say, "I don't

understand the question". At this point many eyes were on me, the translator. Of course, this bugged me and I began to research why Steve
would so stubbornly refuse to answer and started reading all his books
and collecting his articles.

Slowly, with every workshop, I got nosier and started asking Steve
questions, trying not to get on his nerves too much. I think I was quite
shy at this point and, guess what, sometimes he answered. We talked a
little bit about Wittgenstein and the relevant philosophical arguments:
rule following, different usages of the word "to be" and "to know", family
resemblances and then more about cooking (which I was also interested
in . . . but not so much . . . but as I said, I was shy). Insoo was much easier
to talk to at dinners and driving her from workshop A to B – but our
topics were more daily life and chatty and she would shrug off any
mention of philosophy as something Steve was interested in (and I
never quite believed her).

What I owe most to Insoo and Steve is that I regained hope that
people could be helped by conversations and that these conversations
could be respectful and unintrusive. I also regained confidence that
there can be an understanding of "mind" that is consistent, based on
science and that makes sense. For me, this journey was started when I
got to know Insoo and Steve. I was really happy when *More than Miracles*
(de Shazer et al., 2007) came out as it so beautifully summarises and
illustrates this nexus of philosophy and therapy. I'm very grateful for my
rekindled enthusiasm for discovery and research into the questions of
"how can we help people respectfully to develop into the direction of
where they want to go?" and "how can we conceptualise how people use
their minds so that it makes sense?" and "how can both answers fit
together consistently?"

References

De Jong, P., & Berg, I. K. (1997). *Interviewing for Solutions* (1st ed.). Belmont CA: Wadsworth.

de Shazer, S., Dolan, Y. M., Korman, H., Trepper, T. S., McCollum, E. E., & Berg, I. K. (2007). *More than Miracles: The state of the art of solution-focused brief therapy*. Binghamton NY:Haworth Press.

Kirsten Dierolf is the owner and founder of SolutionsAcademy and president of SFCT, the Association for the Quality Development of Solution Focused Consulting and Training.

Yvonne Dolan   Chicago, USA

Hope is in the details, good days and bad days

Hope is in the details

Although we liked to cook together, and frequently spent as much time talking about recipes as therapy, Steve de Shazer and I also had a mutually acknowledged mentor relationship; I literally called him "My Mentor".

About 15 years into our friendship, I risked his annoyance by repeatedly asking, "Steve, where does the concept of hope fit into the solution-focused approach?" The first time I asked, Steve responded that he viewed hope as existing in various specific contexts of experiences and behaviours in which one *feels* hopeful, and thought it was very misleading and likely therapeutically unproductive to try to discuss hope apart from these contexts from which they arose and "lived". He considered it patently ridiculous to try to approach hope as if hope were a "thing" rather than an experience. I politely accepted this explanation, thanked him, and asked the same question again six months later. This time Steve delivered a brief lecture on Wittgenstein during which he quoted several philosophical passages elucidating why, from a therapeutically practical standpoint, it was essential to make a formal distinction between emotions and behaviours, and (again) how feelings like hope could be best and most respectfully, realistically and accurately understood only in the behavioural and experiential contexts in which they arise, ebb, and flow. Again, I thanked him.

A few months later, waiting until Steve was halfway into a frothy mug of ice cold draft beer at the end of the day, I rephrased the question, "Steve, where does hope *live* in the SF approach?" "You're not going to give up on this, are you?" he said wryly and I explained that I couldn't, because I really needed to know. He gave a deep sigh, groaned, and after a few moment of silence, he laughed and answered, "Well, if I absolutely HAD to explain hope in those terms (and apparently I DO in your case) I would say that hope 'lives' in the details of people's exceptions to the problem". This explanation really helped me.

Good Days and Bad Days

Insoo was very gracious in her interactions with clients and seminar participants, and typically maintained a deliberate "one down" stance, which always impressed me as highly adaptive and elegantly therapeutically effective. She characteristically embodied kindness, respectful optimism and gentle serenity, however she also had a lively sense of humour and was also capable of surprising toughness when a situation warranted it. After many years of friendship, co-authoring a book and co-teaching week-long seminars on numerous occasions, I could usually more or less routinely predict Insoo's response to typical questions that came up in SF workshops. But one time she surprised me so much that I almost fell over. Late in the afternoon during a seminar we were teaching together in upstate New York, a participant pointedly asked Insoo how we responded when someone made insulting remarks about the solution-focused approach. Knowing how Insoo usually responded, I anticipated one of her familiar statements about there being many good ways to do effective therapy and that although many people found the SF approach to be useful, she could appreciate that there were many points of view.

However, this time Insoo instead paused for a moment, and then smiling mischievously and with a twinkle in her eyes, answered in a sweet tone of voice, "How I respond to something like that (a derogatory remark about SFBT) would depend on whether I was having a good day, or a bad day. I am a very positive person, and so I rarely have bad days, but if I *was* having a bad day, I suppose I would stop, take a nice deep breath, and then ... I would tell them *to go !#*@! themselves!*"

The entire room of about a hundred seminar participants dissolved into so much laughter that it was several moments before we could continue. On my part, Insoo's statement caused me to laugh so hard that she had to grab me by the arm to prevent me from losing my balance! Insoo was a highly skilled professional, a wise, compassionate confidant, trusted colleague, and a characteristically polite, gracious person; yet she could also be a deeply human, warm hearted and hilariously funny woman friend. It was this especially that I loved about her.

Yvonne Dolan MA is Director of the Institute for Solution-Focused Therapy, Chicago, USA. Specialisms: solution-focused brief therapy and Ericksonian hypnosis. Author of numerous publications. Former president of the Solution-Focused Brief Therapy Association, USA. Yvonne had a particularly close collaboration with Steve de Shazer and Insoo Kim Berg at BFTC Milwaukee, USA.

Heinrich Dreesen   Bremen, Germany

A talking shirt and three oranges

In my memories of Insoo and Steve, the "Love of Three Oranges" runs like a continuous thread through more than two decades of encounters, whereas the T-shirt story was a unique event.

Steve: Talking Shirt

Steve loved surprises and was not afraid to break habitual patterns of interaction. In counselling sessions, he sometimes remained silent for an unexpectedly long time, while on other occasions he posed amazingly concise questions. He could be very direct, reserved or provocative. In general, he seemed more inwardly focused, but if the progress made or the client's good ideas pleased him, he suddenly came alive – for example getting up from his chair, going over to his interlocutor and congratulating him with a firm handshake.

I experienced a very special interruption of a fixed pattern in the mid-90s at our institute, NIK, in Bremen. Steve and I started the morning of the third seminar day for a training group. Using the time-proven questions, we focused attention on what had been interesting, new, helpful and "good" for the participants on the previous day. And what else? And what else? ... Finally, the central question was addressed to our guest from Milwaukee, the founding father of this whole undertaking: "How would you describe the most important thing, the quintessence of your approach?"

Steve hesitated a moment, looked at me, looked around the group of approximately 25 participants, glancing somewhat mischievously, his eyes flashing; pulling his chair a little towards the group, he raised both arms above his head, grabbed his coarse woollen sweater at the collar and began to slowly pull it over his head. Underneath, he was wearing one of his plaid shirts (this time without braces). He put the sweater down carefully at his side, moved forward in his chair again, sat upright and began to undo the top shirt button, then the second, third, etc … All participants fastened their gaze on Steve's hands, curious to see what would happen next. Meanwhile, a red t-shirt began to emerge, with letters printed at the centre, until finally one could read what the big letters spelled out:

SIMPL

The surprise was a complete success – Steve's manner of answering the question was appreciated by everyone in the round: yet another example of minimalism and brevity! Then he told us with the pride of a discoverer how he had purchased this special item of clothing only a few days before in Munich (at the famous art café "Alter Simpl") and was now wearing it for the first time – a premier!

Insoo: Three Oranges

In addition to my work as a psychotherapist, I was, for a long time, a member of the International Jugglers Association (IJA, USA). Even today, I often relax during work breaks by juggling a few minutes for my own pleasure. Particularly when I'm playing with red balls, I remember my very first meeting with Insoo and Steve. In the mid 80s, the couple was invited to a workshop at the Hamburg Institute for Systemic Studies. Before the welcome party, which was held in their honour in the evening, they had taken a walk around the block and bought some healthy victuals: apples, pears and oranges glittered from Insoo's net bag.

The two were obviously in a good mood, so I asked Insoo spontaneously for three oranges. Since we had not yet been introduced, she was a little surprised by my request, but handed me, as curious as she was willing, her finest fruits. One orange followed the other – I started to juggle – initially just for her and Steve, then for everyone in the room. For a few minutes I improvised and tried out different throwing patterns. In this playful fashion we got to know each other, which fortunately also shaped all subsequent encounters.

From the outset we were in agreement that "play" and "pattern breaking" are not only essential to life and learning, but just as much to (therapeutic) work, and in particular the solution-oriented approach to practice and teaching. We repeatedly enjoyed exchanging our experiences with unusual toys, amazing magic and wonderful episodes in (therapeutic) daily life. On occasion, I also performed old and new tricks, preferably with three oranges, sometimes privately, sometimes publicly – whether in our classrooms, in restaurants or at EBTA conferences.

As simple as it may seem when jugglers twirl their objects in the air – it's not easy! "Simple, but not easy" – that's how Steve and Insoo often characterised the solution-oriented work. Because it is not easy – neither for clients nor therapists – to break habits and thought patterns so as to develop new and "more suitable" ones. But the means to achieve this are always there, for life as we currently experience it is nothing but an infinite number of possibilities. Even when juggling, there are countless ways to play – even with three balls.

In this sense, we happily shared ideas about the many possibilities of "less is more" – for example, in terms of our relationship with time. For Steve, the jazz pianists Theolonius Monk and Count Basie were the "masters of omission"; Insoo recounted particular rhythms of her culture. Our solution-oriented approach generates many – and always new – options to pause, decelerate or accelerate with respect to the seconds, minutes, hours, days, weeks and months we spend in counselling and (brief) therapy!

Heinrich Dreesen is a psychotherapist and ritual creator in private practice in Bremen, Germany. He is a trainer and supervisor in solution-focused brief therapy, behavioural therapy and systemic therapy at the North German Institute for Brief Therapy, NIK, and the North German Institute for Behavioural Therapy, NIVT, Bremen. Instructing supervisor and coach (SG). Lecturer at the Centre for Lifelong Learning at the University of Oldenburg.

Wolfgang Gaiswinkler and
Marianne Roessler

Vienna, Austria

Our learning journey

Marianne met Steve de Shazer in 1999 at a seminar in Vienna, which Wolfgang had told her about. He had no time to attend himself, but had read a book by Steve (*Clues*, 1988) and therefore recommended this seminar to her. This first seminar was followed by many more, run by both Insoo and Steve. Initially, Steve's reticent and detached manner towards the seminar participants confused us. It was impressive to see how Steve and Insoo worked with clients. We were soon convinced and captivated by the respectful, competency-based attitude towards the clients that typified this approach and by the linguistic tools it provided. We thus embarked on a solution-focused learning journey that also took us to Milwaukee. Once there, we also got to know a different side of Steve, who was proud to be able to serve up sauerkraut and bratwurst according to an authentic Polish recipe.

First: the medical model and the empowerment model

We invited Insoo to workshops and a course in Vienna and we were able to persuade her to collaborate in a two-year research and implementation project.[1] Among other engagements, she spoke in 2004 at the FH Campus, Vienna, to about 200 social workers. In her talk, she

---

[1] In the context of the EU community initiative jointly financed project from July 2005 to June 2007. We also worked with Insoo on introducing the solution-focused approach at a counselling centre for eviction – for both client work as well as for personnel management. On 15 December 2006 Insoo still held a workshop at the counselling office. On 10 January 2007 she died unexpectedly in Milwaukee – 16 months after Steve died in Vienna.

distinguished between a procedure according to a "medical model" and one based on the systemic solution-focused approach, which follows an "empowerment" model. She highlighted the difference in the following illustration which she drew on an overhead transparency:

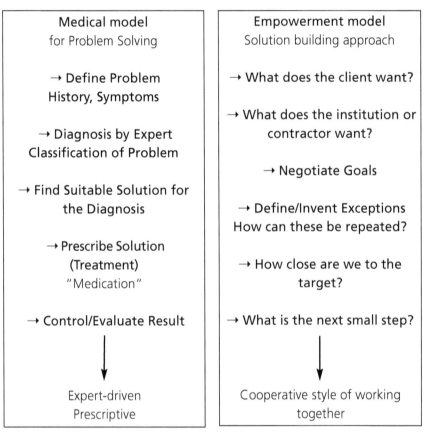

Figure 1: Medical model versus empowerment model

At that moment, a key feature of the solution-focused approach became clear to us. The form of collaboration between client and therapist in these two models differs markedly: in the systemic solution-focused approach it is strictly assumed that people have resources (their own resources and those of their social network) and that solutions can be found by utilising these resources. These resources might not be always immediately tangible for the client, but Insoo made it clear that the task of the professional helper consists primarily in finding solutions in cooperation with the client by adopting a "Not-Knowing" mind set (Gaiswinkler & Roessler, 2009) or inventing solutions (De Jong, Berg & Thielen-Schinder, 1998) and that this goal is best served when the client elaborates, in the most specific terms possible, their desired future. The role of the professional therapist is to assist clients in this endeavour. In contrast, an approach that follows the medical model is expert-controlled: the expertise lies with the professional helpers whose expert knowledge derives a solution from the diagnosis.

At first, we thought that the expertise of professional helpers should not be exploited in the systemic solution-focused approach. Since then, we have come to believe that this view is a misinterpretation of the approach: expert knowledge can, of course, be useful in the professional helper-client intervention (de Shazer et al., 2007, p. 155), such as in demonstrating the not-knowing attitude, for example, by asking questions and making an offer. The solution-focused approach emphasises the freedom of choice: to what extent the knowledge offered is helpful – and what importance is attached to it – lies entirely with the client.

We remember a conversation at our kitchen table with Insoo. She said that, of course, she would offer ideas. For example, if she asked a mother, "When did you last feed your baby vegetables?" This question contains information, namely, that it is good to give babies vegetables. Insoo then said, "Of course I sometimes tell the clients my ideas but they decide what is helpful". Insoo pointed out that it was not a matter of never offering knowledge and information, but merely that it is a matter for professional decision, whether, when and in what form we do so. Once, when discussing the question as to how SFBT differed from other treatments, an experienced practising solution-focused therapist said that in this type of therapy the client is given no advice. This prompted Insoo Kim Berg to ask in astonishment, "What? You think that if you knew something that could help the client, you would not tell him?" (de Shazer et al., 2007, p. 155)[2]

---

[2] See also the article quoted in the next section on micro-analysis.

In the realm of social work in which we are often involved, but also in many other contexts, making expert knowledge available is often an essential aspect of the work (legal claims, institutional resources etc.). One reason for this may be that the client explicitly wants to hear our opinion and professional advice. Another reason may be that our contract or ethical considerations require that we contribute our expertise. One approach that follows the empowerment model shows that the expertise of not-knowing is a prerequisite in order to proceed, if necessary, in an expert-driven manner. What do we mean by the expertise of not-knowing in an expert-controlled context? If we do not know what the clients want and what goals they have, we as professional helpers cannot know how to steer the on-going process together with the client, nor can we know what information might be important for the client. This applies even more to work with clients in a compulsory context. In contexts where the professional person has been enlisted to make a decision that may be contrary to the wishes of the client, such as the protection of minors in the case of child welfare or in the context of leadership in organisations, our expertise and assessment can play a significant role such that we can reasonably apply the "medical model" or aspects of it. What we have learned from Insoo is that the question regarding what the client wants and what is important to her cannot be answered by experts, but only by the client, who is the expert of their own life and of their frame of reference. In situations and circumstances in which our expertise is in demand, the empowerment model should always be applied to define interventions. The professional temptation, to think that we know better than the client what is good for them, must be constantly resisted. At the very heart of the medical model – in medicine itself – this idea is now being discussed at the highest levels under the title of *shared decision-making*.

This model, as sketched by Insoo and extended in the ideas mentioned above, helped us and is now helping our students and seminar participants to understand that the "expertise of not-knowing", and thus the empowerment model, should provide the framework for any professional help; with this not-knowing attitude we help clients, firstly, to develop ideas of a desired future and we use the not-knowing attitude to control the use of expert knowledge, adapted to the clients' specific objectives. Insoo explained it simply as follows: "I am not an expert on the client's life". And in the same vein: "It's simple but not easy; we have to learn how to change a complaint into a goal and we have to look for very small exceptions and broaden them" (Insoo Kim Berg, lecture on 22 October 2004 in Vienna: Roessler / Gaiswinkler 2011).

The learning journey continues

Second: a different view of relationship work

Insoo taught us a different perspective on the issue of industrial relations: a common mistake criticised by Insoo is that professional helpers assume that a relationship with the client must first be built in order to get or even coerce them to do certain things. Insoo said, "That's nonsense and leads to burnout". A good relationship is created according to Insoo when, from the very beginning right to the end of the helper-client interaction, I allow myself to be led by the following questions:

- What is important to the client?
- Who is important to the client?
- What is the client willing to do?
- What is the client capable of?

Relationship building is a continuous process in which the client's goals are explored and referred to throughout. If these stand in conflict with the corporate contract, labour relations are developed in such a manner that the objectives of the client and those of the institution are negotiated **transparently.**

We are convinced (and it is regarded as common sense in scientific debate and has been confirmed in many studies) that the quality of the working alliance is central for successful collaboration. Steve told us over dinner at a Korean restaurant in Vienna, how he met Insoo and cooked for her, and also that NLP students had once asked him how he managed to create such a strong rapport with his clients. Steve replied that he did not create the rapport but got involved as soon as the client's goals were the focus of attention and the attempt was made to discover what they really wanted, and that it was simply a matter of not destroying the rapport during such a conversation. He thus held the same view as Insoo that in working with clients it can never be a matter of establishing a rapport in order to talk the clients into doing something.

Third: the attitude of curiosity – Insoo's curiosity about clients

We will never forget how relentlessly Insoo asked her clients to find or invent answers: she fixed the clients with an interested look that clearly signalled, "I'm waiting for an answer, and I know that you can give an answer". Her persistence almost "forced" answers, for example, when she said, "I am confused!" or after clients had described to her their difficult, hopeless situation, she continued with the question, "So, what are you going to do?" And then with her interested gaze allowed for a long pause and waited for an answer.

Fourth: make a difference with each sequence in a communication

After Steve's death, Insoo stayed with us in our little guest room whenever she was in Vienna.[3] During her last visit in December 2006, she told us about an informal workshop with Janet Bavelas on "micro-analysis" which she herself had proposed, which was to take place in Canada in the summer of 2007. Unfortunately, Insoo was not

---

[3] For Insoo this arrangement was handy because our office is next to the apartment and she could use it any time before and after the workshops, as she always did, early in the morning and in the evening. We often asked ourselves how she could work so much.

to participate. However, as she had intended, the people she had spoken to met up with Janet Bavelas on Vancouver Island in the summer of 2007. This meeting opened a new door for us into the world of micro-analysis. This builds on a consideration which Steve had formulated in 1997: "Ever since I (de Shazer) began practising brief therapy in the early 1970s, my 'research' question was, 'What do therapists do that is useful?' In the 1980s, we changed this to: 'What do clients and therapists do together that is useful?'" (de Shazer & Berg, 1997, p. 122). Since then, we have watched recordings of our own consultations and supervisions, as well as videotapes of Insoo and Steve again and again, asking ourselves, for example, "Which sequence in the conversation is taken up and developed, which sequence is discarded, how is what is said (non)verbally supported?" Or we discuss "Where does this question lead?", "What could have been the backdrop?", "What answers do clients give after a pause when they had initially replied, 'I don't know'?", "When does the consultant interrupt?" Or, for example, "When does the consultant allow himself to be interrupted, and when not?" The analysis of client-helper conversations enables us to look more closely at what we are really doing; since then we have learned to refine and hone our view and understand communication as a co-construction.[4]

Fifth: "What have you learned from your clients?"

Steve asked repeatedly at the beginning of each course workshop in Bremen at NIK what the participants had learned from their clients since the last time they met. At that time we did not really understand the question. Today we know that if we manage to learn from our clients what is helpful for them we can support each client and at the same time

---

[4] (Bavelas, 2000a), "Moment by moment, the therapist and the client(s) (co)create a version of the problem and its solutions. [So] we must examine all therapeutic communication on a micro-level, even down to the word or phrase." And this led Janet to the conclusion that we need to use language just as carefully and cautiously as the surgeon wields a scalpel. (Bavelas, 2000b).

develop our expertise. And this question, we believe today, did not arise by chance; after all, many tools (such as the miracle question and scaling questions) were introduced into the conversation by clients. The team from Milwaukee was smart enough to take up these impulses, to experiment with them systematically and turn them into standard solution-focused tools.

The solution-focused approach is much more than a set of tools, because what matters most is the underlying attitude. It is not, therefore, so much about using all the tools as treating the instruments as a toolbox: "You have a lot of tools in your toolbox; you decide what you use" (Insoo Kim Berg at the Vienna workshop, 2006). The tools helped us at the beginning to understand and implement the approach and they help us still to make it measurable.

Finally

The most important thing we have learned over the years, and which shapes our work, is that people can always be considered from different sides; we can describe one and the same person as competent or as deficient. The solution-focused approach helps us in our daily work to find the skills, strengths and abilities *together* with the clients.

Even after their deaths, both Insoo and Steve heavily influence our work and further learning journey: we analyse conversations more carefully and differently, we conduct research in this area, and we experiment in our interventions with the knowledge that the expertise concerning the client's life lies with them. We are firmly convinced (also on the basis of much scientific evidence) that the most important task for professional helpers consists in helping clients to discover their strengths and coping strategies. In conclusion, to give Insoo the final say: "This approach means we are listening for different things and we are always looking for an opportunity to help the client to become more self-sufficient," and elsewhere she said, "The client's own goal drives the activities". (Insoo Kim Berg, workshop in Vienna, December 2006.)

With Insoo and Steve we have discovered an exciting way to assist clients in developing and achieving their goals and for this we thank them heartily! Often when we are not clear about something we say to each other, "What a pity that we can no longer ask them".

References

Bavelas, J. B., Coates, L., & Johnson, T. (2000a). Listeners as Co-Narrators. *Journal of Personality and Social Psychology, 79,* 941–952.

Bavelas, J. B., McGee, D., Phillips, B., & Routledge, R. (2000b). Micro-analysis of Communication in Psychotherapy. *Human Systems: The Journal of Systemic Consultation & Management, 11,* 47–66.

De Jong, P., Berg, I. K., & Theilen-Schindler, K. (1998). Lösungen (er)finden. Das Werkstattbuch der lösungsorientierten Kurztherapie. 2. Aufl. Dortmund: Verl. Modernes Lernen (Systemische Studien, 17)

de Shazer, S. and Berg, I. K. (1997). What works in Therapy? Remarks on Research Aspects in Solution Brief Therapy. *Journal of Family Therapy and Systemic Practice, 19,* 121–124.

de Shazer, S., Dolan, Y., Korman, H., Trepper T., McCullum, E. and, Berg, I. K. (2007). *More Than Miracles. The State of the Art of Solution-Focused Brief Therapy* . Binghamton NY: The Haworth Press.

Gaiswinkler, W., & Roessler M. (no date) Die KlientInnen fühlen sich oft ohnmächtig, aber wir sehen sie als ExpertInnen für ihr Leben: h t t p : / / w w w . n e t z w e r k - o s t . a t / p u b l i k a t i o n e n / p d f /publikationen_klientinnenalsexpertinnen.pdf Last checked on 01.10.2011.

Gaiswinkler, W., & Roessler, M. (2009). Using the expertise of knowing and the expertise of not-knowing to support processes of empowerment in social work practice. *Journal of Social Work Practice, 23,* 215–227.

Marianne Roessler DSA Mag is a social worker, social scientist, supervisor, instructional supervisor and organisational consultant in private practice. Network Partner of OS'T – Network for Social Research – Organisational Consulting – Supervision – Training.

Wolfgang Gaiswinkler Mag is a social scientist, supervisor, and organisational consultant in private practice. Network partner OS'T – Network for Social Research – Organisational Consulting – Supervision – Training.

Evan George   London, UK

"Just a bunch of talk"

I have a memory of when I first met Steve de Shazer. Many years have passed and I cannot be sure what relationship my memory has with anything an observer might have noticed on the day. But my memory, my version, is important to me and I would not want to be 'put right' by any of the others present on that day.

The time was May 1990. Chris Iveson, Harvey Ratner and I had got interested in solution focused brief therapy in 1986 and had set up a project to test and to evaluate the approach in the British National Health Service in 1987. Our enthusiasm grew and grew, and in 1989 we found the courage to ring Steve de Shazer one evening from London to ask him to come to present a two-day conference on the approach, and while he was in London to come to spend a clinical afternoon with our team and to deliver a lecture in the morning to our, rather doubtful, multi-disciplinary colleagues. To our joy and amazement Steve indicated that he would be happy to come to London and a date was agreed in the spring of 1990. Chris, Harvey and I were, at the time, working in a leading British systemic therapy clinic, a rather academic institution staffed by a team who were engaged in teaching at the cutting edge of "family therapy" throughout the UK and indeed more widely. The clinic, in other words, took itself and its thinking seriously.

So the day that I was first to meet the man whose writings had inspired my work over the previous three years was a day of huge signifi-cance. And what do I think that I remember as Steve arrived? Was he really wearing a big, thick, checked lumberjack shirt? Could he really have been wearing a pair of wide braces holding up his jeans? And would anyone have come to our clinic to deliver a key-note lecture wearing black monkey boots? But that is what I remember. And did

Steve really, when invited to stand up and open his lecture to a challenging and largely sceptical audience, read off a flip-chart the three rules of solution focused practice:

- If it ain't broke don't fix it.
- If it works do more of it.
- If it doesn't work do something different.

And yet now I would never want to be told that my memory did not "really" happen because this memory represents for me the challenge that solution focused brief therapy posed to the (over)-intellectualised world that systemic therapy had come to inhabit, a world in which everything from quantum physics, to the new biology, to Taoism and Alice in Wonderland had been used to offer novel metaphors to open up new perspectives and new possibilities for the work. Therapy, Steve was soon to remind us, "was just a bunch of talk" and what's more "a bunch of talk" that could easily be learnt. Indeed in *Clues* (de Shazer, 1988) Steve went so far as to offer us a process map of the approach, thereby reducing the complexity of the decision-making that faced us as therapists. It is simple he seemed to suggest; if x happens just do y, but if z happens try b. Were we not, Steve seemed to be asking, getting a little self-important, a little over-impressed with our own cleverness, somewhat over-excited by the world of ideas that were perhaps beginning to seem more real and more important to us than the mundane problems, the routine unhappiness that many of our clients presented? The lumberjack shirt, the braces, jeans and boots of my "memory" brought us down to earth with a bump – just a "bunch of talk" – something that we all do.

And yet we therapists, we are a restless bunch, never satisfied, always looking for new ways to think about what we do, new descriptions, new distinctions, new metaphors, new ways of marking our territory, new ways of building our empires. And so even we, the solution focused simpletons, indeed even Steve, moved away from the radicalism of Ockham's Razor and began to talk about post-modernism, social constructionism and radical constructivism, "what is the difference, we wondered"; we (tried to) ~~read~~ or misread Derrida and Foucault, we struggled to get to grips with Wittgenstein and in so doing we provided our model with the complexity that brings respect, academic respect and acceptance in that world beyond our own. But is any of this necessary? Does any of this make us better therapists? Who knows – if we keep on this track before long we will be able to hold our heads high when meeting other therapists, we will again have a model that the general public will admiringly not understand. Unlike my memory of Steve in 1990 we will look just like all the rest.

Reference

de Shazer, S. (1988). *Clues: Investigating Solutions in Brief Therapy.* New York: Norton.

Evan George MA, MSc is a solution focused brief therapist, coach, trainer, consultant and supervisor working at BRIEF in London, UK.

Wallace J Gingerich   Cleveland, USA

Observing what works

In 1983 Steve de Shazer, Michele Weiner Davis and I began meeting weekly in what we loosely called "the research group". Steve was the theoretician, Michele was the clinician, and I was the researcher. Our goal was to come up with research questions that would help us understand what makes SFBT work, pure and simple. We met behind the mirror or in Steve's office, observing live cases or videos to ground our discussions, sometimes fuelled by a couple of pieces of Panda licorice.

To learn more about what worked, we decided to look at videotapes of good interviews to see if we could actually see or hear what it was that made them good. Good interviews were those in which the client showed evidence of change. Once we were able to define and observe client change we looked at the therapists to see what they did that was related to the client change.

After a few months of trying out different definitions and coding schemes we agreed on one that broke down the interview transcript into "thought units" and then coded the content of each thought unit. For clients, the content codes basically reduced to "change talk" or not. We coded client change talk when clients described positive changes in their problem or situation, talked about what they would like to do differently, or talked about their situation in a different way that indicated a positive shift in their construction of their situation. This led to an interesting "discovery" one afternoon as we were training students to use the coding system. We were observing an interview segment that Steve coded as "client change talk" but I did not. We went back over it several times, trying to figure out what explained our different codings when suddenly it dawned on us – the client was describing change, but she didn't recognise it as such. In other words, it was "unrecognised change".

Once we could code the client's change talk we focused on the therapists, and we came up with four codes for them: asking the clients what changes they noticed, asking them to explain and amplify those changes, complimenting them for their changes, and asking what else they would do to keep the change going. I was a little embarrassed at our coding scheme – it seemed so simple and unsophisticated – yet, we found that indeed client change talk did clearly follow therapists' questions about change. That seems rather obvious now, but at the time it seemed like an important discovery – I guess we were still getting used to looking on the surface of things.

With the help of social work students from the University of Wisconsin Milwaukee we coded a cross section of 20-30 interviews, including a variety of first, second and subsequent sessions, and a variety of therapists, including therapists who weren't practising the BFTC approach. When we looked at those videos of good sessions we could clearly see that clients were doing a lot of talking about change (whereas they weren't in poor videos), and the therapists were doing a lot of asking about and reinforcing it. As the study went on we found ourselves using the term "change talk" more and more, not only in our research but in our practice as well. Our little study was telling us that what mattered was talk about change – simple as that. We found change talk to be a good barometer for how the interview was going – lots of change talk meant it was a good interview; not much change talk meant it was a poor interview.

When we graphed the amount of change talk during the course of the sessions we noticed a strikingly pronounced pattern; initial sessions contained little if any "change talk" whereas subsequent sessions included a lot of change talk, usually about half of all of the talk. We also noticed that sessions conducted by non-BFTC therapists contained little change talk in any of the sessions.

This was amazing, and in our quest to be as brief and non-intrusive as possible it was obvious what we needed to do – we needed to lop off the first session and begin with the second. First sessions contained no change talk and therefore they were useless. But, how could we begin an initial session with a client by asking "what has changed?" Clients expect to be asked about the problem, how long it has been going on, how bad it is, etc., etc., and would think questions about change were inappropriate and missed the point.

Steve and Michele and I spent at least a few weeks trying to figure out how we could get the conversation in the first interview focused on change without the client thinking we weren't interested in their problem or were simply off the track. We came up with some fairly wacky ideas, like saying we were conducting a research project and before we get started we would like to ask you what you have noticed recently that indicates the problem is getting better. We weren't really coming up with anything that we thought would work, however.

Then Michele came in one day all excited saying, "Guys, you'll never believe what happened to me last week". She had been conducting an initial interview with the mother of a teenage boy who was getting in trouble in school and midway through the interview the woman interrupted Michele and asked, "Would you like to know what I have been trying so far?" Michele was taken aback, to say the least, but managed to get her wits about her and say yes, of course she was interested. The mother went on to describe three concrete things she had started doing in the past week, and Michele followed up by asking how it was working, which led to an extended period of change talk, right there in the initial session!

Although Michele's experience was unplanned, a "therapeutic accident" as we called it, it happened in a receptive context where we had been thinking about change talk and first interviews. This no doubt helped Michele take note of the event and follow where it led in the interview, and we took advantage of her experience to push the development of SFBT one step further. As always, we tried to see if we could make the same "accident" happen in subsequent initial sessions, and lo and behold we found it could be done! Often all that was needed was a simple lead-in such as, "Before we get into more details about the problem, I'm curious to know if you have noticed any times in the last week or so when the problem hasn't happened, or when things have been a little better".

These discoveries, that change talk was what mattered, that first interviews included little or no change talk, and that change talk could in fact happen in first interviews, all had a marked impact on our subsequent practice – we became more and more solution-focused. These were very heady times for us at BFTC, and I will always think of those years as some of the most creative and exhilarating years of my career. It would not have happened for me without the inquisitive, creative and pioneering spirit that Steve and Insoo fostered, and I shall always be grateful to them for the opportunity they gave me to be a part of their team.

Wallace J Gingerich is Professor Emeritus, Case Western Reserve University, Cleveland, Ohio, USA.

Joachim Hesse   Euskirchen, Germany

The miracle question as the beginning of a potentially wonderful healing

I want to keep the memory of the practice of Insoo and Steve alive with the help of Jorge Semprun's question: "Is there a miracle without wounds?" (Gstrein & Semprun, 2001). To this end, I will use a central theme of theirs concerning the miracle question.

True to Steve and Insoo's motto, "If it doesn't work, do something else", I argue for a recommendation-based use of the miracle question. Depending on what turns up (or is recommended) during the conversation, i.e. picking up on whatever is best suited and helpful for a particular client, the original miracle question (points 1–2) could first be employed and then, as needed, followed by variations that are framed in terms of the consultant's recommendation (point 3).

1) Let me ask you an unusual question . . . a question for which you need time . . . that is perhaps unusual (uncommon, unconventional) . . .
2) Imagine . . . you're at home . . . it is night . . . and you go to sleep . . . and while you sleep . . . a miracle occurs . . . and the problems (feelings) that were the reason for your coming here. . . disappear. Because you are sleeping . . . you do not notice . . . that a miracle has happened . . . You wake up the next morning . . . how exactly do you realise . . . that a miracle has happened? [I'll omit the other usual follow-up questions and come directly to the variations on the theme.]
3) What is different after the miracle?
   – What deep desire has been fulfilled?
   – Which (current, past) conflicts have been resolved?
   – Which open wounds (e.g. personally experienced wounds,

injuries, stress, impairments, slights, crises, degradations, humiliations, indignities, threats, etc.) were healed or resolved after the miracle?

- Following the miracle, which feelings of hurt do you take seriously and allow room for?
- Which ignored needs (for example the need for intimacy and pleasure, self-respect and self-assurance, firm commitment and togetherness or for isolation and withdrawal, freedom to express needs and feelings) do you recognise and acknowledge after the miracle?
- Which existing wounds can you begin to accept?
- Following the miracle, what aspects of your needs, goals and objectives do you acknowledge that you can start to address, step for step?
- Theme 1: Basic wounds/injuries (but by no means just this kind) should be recognised so that they can form the seed for a new basis for living.
- Theme 2: Injuries can be healed if they are recognised.

Particularly following extreme, critical life events, if those chronic wounds that are so acute and immediate can be addressed and acknowledged in the miracle question, then they can be used as turning points. The acknowledgement of previously suppressed wounds often leads to tears. The tears that are shed acknowledge wounds that were hitherto ignored, so these wounds can now heal; and neglected needs can emerge again. Open wounds can be a source of strength if they are not ignored due to a fixation with the solution as, for example, in the unrelenting search for "resources".

Instead of a pathological rejection, I plead for a wholesome, compassionate attention and appreciative reconciliation to the wounds inflicted by life. They are relevant aspects – often they assume important protective functions along the path towards life and the solution – and cry out to be included. If the miracle question can attach significance to these open wounds, a wonderful healing can begin.

The idea is not to avoid what is painful and threatening, nor to endure it resignedly or wage war against it in an over-compensating manner. Insofar as the client agrees to a suitable recommendation, this means starting towards a meaningful, healing reconciliation, following Helm Stierlin –who Steve de Shazer once told me understood most about the solution-oriented approach.

It seems to me that Steve and Insoo's code of practice touchingly reconciled both poles of wounded astonishment, such that the seeds of a surprised recognition of wounds could grow and flourish.

Reference

Gstrein, N., & Semprun, J. (2001). *What was and what is.* London: Routledge.

Joachim Hesse is a psychologist, psychotherapist, educational therapist and supervisor.

Debbie Hogan
Singapore, Singapore

A lasting legacy

I was first introduced to solution focused brief therapy in Singapore when I attended a counsellors' support group in the early 1990s. Someone showed a video of Insoo Kim Berg working with an alcoholic. I was intrigued because she never addressed his drinking problem but instead asked what he wanted from the session. I decided to investigate this strange and different approach. It couldn't have been more different from how I had been trained. My previous experience in the United States had been with psychiatric institutions where progress and improvement were slow and often discouraging. I was ready to try something new and different. I saw myself as a "jack of all trades and master of none".

My search led me to reading books by Steve de Shazer (like *Keys to Solution in Brief Therapy,* de Shazer, 1985), Milton Erickson and the Mental Research Institute group. I decided to go to Milwaukee to study with Insoo and Steve. As luck would have it, they came to Singapore in the late 90s. I attended a two-day workshop on solution focused brief therapy. Insoo did a live demo and her questions intrigued me. Steve and Insoo were such interesting trainers. They had very different training styles yet complimented each other. It was fascinating to watch them work.

I was smitten by SF work and talked with Insoo about going to Milwaukee. She convinced me to take a new and innovative program she was starting in Singapore in 2000. I never regretted it. It was intensive and rigorous with over 250 hours of training, 84 hours of supervision and lasted a year and a half. Insoo included other international trainers. It was an amazing opportunity to learn from some of the best in the field. I became good friends with some of the trainers, like Insoo herself, Brian Cade, Therese Steiner, Arild Aambø and later

Yvonne Dolan, Terry Trepper, Mark McKergow, Jenny Clarke, Peter Szabó, Chris Iveson and Harry Korman. A new world opened up for me as I became part of the international community of solution focused practitioners. I discovered a group of people who were generous, respectful and collaborative.

Insoo's unique way of training and responding to questions was magical. We observed her in therapy through a one-way mirror. She made it look so easy. We struggled to learn it and she encouraged us to try small steps. She told us "It's easy to learn but hard to do".

I realised I had finally found what I was looking for and decided to focus on the solution focused approach. I began noticing positive changes. I witnessed transformation in my clients. Many said "I have hope again". I had not heard that before. The number of sessions reduced and sometimes after one session clients were satisfied. I was convinced I was on the right track. The approach was refreshing and respectful, highlighted client strengths and focused on what they wanted. As a therapist I was conscientious and thought I had to be the expert on the issue. Insoo said, "If you are working harder than the client there is something wrong". I was relieved to hear that. But it wasn't easy to shift from my problem-focused, pathology-based orientation.

I became concerned with where solution focused brief therapy was heading in Singapore. I would hear other therapists say, "Solution focused brief therapy doesn't work". They had read a book or taken a workshop and abandoned the approach because it was ineffective. I decided I wanted to develop a community of solution focused practitioners who believed in its effectiveness and had the benefit of good training.

In 2004 the Academy of Solution Focused Training was established. I used a similar model of training that Insoo developed and we invited international trainers. Insoo was our keynote speaker at our 1st Asia Pacific Solution Focused Approach Conference in 2006. I told her how much she had influenced me, not knowing that it would be my last chance to express my appreciation. I told her she had revolutionised my practice and changed me forever.

This approach has expanded beyond Singapore across Asia and

continues to grow. Singapore is a regional hub for commerce, banking and multi-national companies and ideally situated for even more expansion and growth. It's exciting to see the calibre of practitioners who are now part of our solution focused community. Our monthly Peer Supervision group is in its third year and our conferences continue to draw people who practise this approach.

At one point when things became very difficult Insoo encouraged me to keep going. She really wanted things to go well in Singapore. We began to work on our next conference for July 2007. We exchanged quite a few emails in the next few months, even the night before she died. Brian Cade called me the next day to give me the news. On January 10, 2007 Insoo passed away. It was such a shock to lose her so unexpectedly.

The personal impact of Insoo continues to give me inspiration and hope. We shared a special affinity because we were born in Korea. She asked me how I came to live in the United States and I felt she was one of the few people who understood it. I was a product of the Korean War as my biological father was an American soldier and my biological mother was Korean. I was abused and neglected and eventually abandoned. I was found living on the streets of Seoul and taken to an orphanage. I was part of the first group of international adoptees from Korea sent to America on an army aircraft. I began my new life at five years old and was adopted by an American family. These early childhood experiences often left me depressed, suicidal and struggling to fit in this world.

When I met Insoo and learned about the solution focused approach, my life started shifting for the better. The narrative, the memories, the experiences began to have a different meaning. My past became a resource and what I perceived as inadequacies became opportunities. My journey of self-discovery and transition into a more hopeful future enabled me to use this as a resource rather than being a victim of my past. Insoo had a strong belief in people and their innate abilities. This belief lead to self-belief and confidence and opened up possibilities for me that I never thought possible. It was transformational.

One of my trainees told me about a student she had been working with. The student was failing in school, depressed and thinking of quitting school. Eventually the student graduated top of his class and, during his graduating address to his class, thanked this lecturer and told her that she was his "guardian angel". The lecturer then told me that I was *her* guardian angel. We may never know the full extent and far-reaching implications of our influence. For me, Insoo was a guiding light and wise guide. Her influence in Asia and certainly in Singapore has been and continues to be huge. It was her hope to take solution focused brief therapy into Singapore. She has left such an important legacy.

Reference

de Shazer, S. (1985). *Keys to Solution in Brief Therapy.* New York: WW Norton.

Debbie Hogan BS, MS is a psychotherapist, trainer and coach, Singapore, Republic of Singapore, where she leads the Academy of Solution Focused Training.

Svea van der Hoorn   Cape Town, South Africa

Tragedy excavating to compost-making: A journey that grew from reading Minimal Elegance by Steve de Shazer

I stumbled across Steve's words not because I was looking for them, but while I was searching for materials for the family therapy course that I offered as part of the Masters in Educational Psychology Programme I was co-ordinating. This was 1989, and my stumble was not the nowadays familiar Google-assisted stumble. This stumble happened in the university library amongst the journal possibilities. The title attracted me – *Minimal Elegance*. My response – "This sounds like someone who understands that life lived aesthetically becomes a creative activity no matter how difficult and challenging the circumstances." I also liked the "minimal". Living in South Africa in the late 1980s was anything but minimal. We were drowning in complexities and ambiguities. The idea that someone had written an article expressing the possibility that minimal was enough to achieve elegance drew me to the pages. Within moments of starting to read, I experienced a freshness of thinking accompanied by a vista of possibilities unfurling to far future horizons.

What did I notice that told me that this was something different, something worth pursuing?

"Brief therapists are often told that they are simple-minded. This, I gather, is meant as a put-down, but, as a brief therapist, I consider it a profound compliment."

These opening words started a curiosity and an appreciation which is still continuing after more than 21 years. Studying psychology, especially at post-graduate level, had made me aware of what awe and reverence was offered to the complex and the deep. For me, the language of psychology was more often used to construct complication than describe complexity, to obscure rather than illuminate depth.

"No matter how complex the description, the intervention should still be the simplest possible."

Living in South Africa where roads were strewn with burning tyres, and school children ran to beat the approaching kaspirs (armoured troop carriers) rather than to beat one another in athletics competitions, trauma was plentiful. Access to services was minimal. Might this brief approach offer something worthwhile and do-able in what seemed an impossible and intractable situation? The pragmatism was delightfully reassuring – in the mundane, the creative and life-affirming can dwell, so look for it.

I put some of this to work at a family mental health clinic at a local day hospital where people described their problems in everyday language – "I don't know where my 14 year old son is. He's been missing for 3 months. I can't sleep. I cry all the time. I just need to know if he is safe". We, the staff, transformed this poignancy into textbook speak and formulation structures – we amplified the stuckness. And, as we moved from their everyday descriptions of distress to the comfort of our psychobabble, we alienated ourselves and declared ourselves unequipped to act resourcefully together with them in their quests. She didn't want us to fix her multigenerational transmission issues of abandonment, nor her attachment issues, she just wanted to know if her child was safe. After a few SFB questions, she told us she hoped to manage each long anguish-filled night and each long weary day better, even if she couldn't know whether her child was safe.

So what did *Minimal Elegance* say about meeting these complaints of apparent intractable stuckness?

"No matter how complicated the description of the problem or the (apparent) duration, brief therapists believe that a small and simple difference that is noticed will often lead to unpredictably large changes."

Aha; illumination. I knew about the butterfly effect and now had a glimpse of how to do our talk with clients differently. How might I talk with them so that my words might act like the flap of a butterfly's wings, not to set off a tidal wave, but to develop energising and hope-filled descriptions of moments connected to a better future?

"Seek a difference that makes a difference."

Might this help me answer the fraught question about what services might be perceived as welcome and helpful by clients as well as satisfy the growing bureaucratic clamour for using evidence-based practice? Here was a way of practising developed from evidence – it honoured the lives of clients by taking seriously that they knew better than what might make the kind of difference that would take them from feeling stuck to having possibilities for moving forward in their lives.

"Simple interventions do not often come about spontaneously. They take time and a lot of thought." "While it looks simple, it is not easy."

These words were very comforting. So, this way of working might look simple but would demand a lot. A post-graduate programme in psychology is about developing humility. It is not about acquiring new knowledge. We assumed that the carefully selected few who embark on this journey have more than sufficient book knowledge, and more than sufficient cleverness. What we looked for were signs of developing wisdom. *Minimal Elegance* forthrightly confessed the shock at the realisation that clients already had the beginnings of a solution in their repertoires. Doing the therapy job wisely became a quest to develop resource hearing ears and possibility spotting eyes, complemented by a language for conversations of difference. We were to engage in a creative dance of exploring possibilities, no matter how dire the circumstances clients reported.

And, just to add a stretch – the stringent discipline of being willing to change one's maps was necessary. Sweep in all the evidence emerging from sessions, rather than assigning any data that didn't fit as due to chance or random error. Routinely discarded pieces of clients' conversations now became critical material. *Minimal Elegance* introduced me to the proposal that as therapists we can choose to become compost makers rather than tragedy excavators. When amongst the debris, we can shine light on that which has potential and can be useful to help people grow a better life. Compost makers hold an unwavering belief in the creative capacity of living beings to survive. They use language deliberately to evoke the horizon of flourishing. This is simple, but decidedly not easy.

And so began my exploration of using solution-focused brief therapy with individuals, families and groups – a language journey which continues to invigorate, inspire and delight. Years after my paper-based encounter, I was privileged to see Steve at work on video and in person, and to witness how words can be the magic that makes a difference. I am deeply humbled and grateful for how his words encouraged me to have thoughts of my own, thoughts which enabled us in developing lives connected to being at our best. More recently, my explorations have expanded into the territory of brief coaching – but that is another story.

Extracts from de Shazer, S. (1986). Minimal Elegance. The Family Therapy Networker, Sept./Oct., 57–60.

A Pantoum* of Appreciation

? Steve's curiosity and irreverence – refreshingly enlivening, respectful

♥ A cloverleaf gift that emboldens my heart

🐝 Abundance of Insoo's productivity – leave no footprints, only flowers

👊 Dust to dust … And still their words invite attention.

♥ A cloverleaf gift that emboldens my heart

👍 ☺ WOWW! Working on what works can make a difference

👊 Dust to dust … And still their words invite our attention

𝄢 Words were originally magic – so said Steve, borrowed from Freud.

👍 ☺ WOWW! Working on what works does make a difference

♀ Illuminate, magnify and liberate the possibilities in everyday detail

𝄢 Words were originally magic – so said Steve, borrowed from Freud

☞ Clues, keys, patterns – it is simple, but not easy.

♀ Illuminate, magnify and liberate the possibilities in everyday detail

🐝 Abundance of Insoo's productivity – leave no footprints, only flowers

☞ Clues, keys, patterns – it remains simple, but not easy

? Steve's curiosity and irreverence – refreshingly enlivening, respectful.

👍 ☺ WOW!

Dr Svea van der Hoorn D.Ed is an educational psychologist, solution-focused brief coach, therapist and trainer based in Cape Town, South Africa. Working in South Africa, UK, Europe, Australia, Singapore. International Faculty member of SolutionSurfers, Switzerland.

---

*A pantoum is a form of poetry with repeating lines throughout the poem. It is composed of a series of quatrains; the second and fourth lines of each stanza are repeated as the first and third lines of the next.

Michael F Hoyt   San Rafael, California, USA

Remembering Steve de Shazer and Insoo Kim Berg

first met Steve in December 1988 at the Erickson Brief Therapy conference in San Francisco. We were in the lobby of the hotel where the conference was being held. Moshe Talmon, who had done some training at BFTC in Milwaukee, introduced us. I invited Steve and the group he was with to a party we were having at my house in a couple of days. He accepted and attended, bringing with him a number of folks.

Over the years we shared meals in lots of places: at his and Insoo's home in Milwaukee; in restaurants in New York, Milwaukee, San Francisco, and Phoenix; at an outdoor noodle stand by the river in Fukuoka, southern Japan. We always had a good time – bright conversation, humour, sports talk, jazz, food, politics – and sometimes something more personal. Steve was nine years my senior, and I felt, in addition to our friendly collegial interests, something of a big brother-little brother connection.

I read almost all of Steve's writing, of course, and was delighted that he read some of mine. I once served as host for a couple of days when he was teaching a workshop in San Francisco, and I sat on the stage and helped moderate a discussion between Steve and Michael White when BFTC sponsored a two-day "Narrative Solutions/Solution Narratives" conference in Milwaukee in 1996. Steve also graciously participated in two long interviews that we did for publication (Hoyt, 1994, 1996), one with his mentor John Weakland at the 1992 Erickson conference held in Phoenix, and the other in 1994 with his wife and professional partner, Insoo Berg, in Steve's BFTC office – they are both reprinted in my book *Interviews with Brief Therapy Experts* (Hoyt, 2001).

Steve and Insoo's development of solution-focused therapy, which has greatly influenced me, signalled a profound shift from the usual therapy approach based on pathology to one based on fundamental respect for clients' values and competence. This major contribution is consistent with the way Steve and Insoo were in the world, taking people at face value, letting them be themselves. As Steve explained in the 1992 interview we did with his mentor, John Weakland, "[E]very session is somehow a unique event, and the main thing that the therapist has to do is listen and keep it simple. And if you do it, I think, the clients will tell you what to do ... It's good to know what doesn't work, but it's really helpful to know what does".

Steve was Steve. As I got to know him, I came to realise that he was somewhat shy and not overly concerned with social niceties. One time I arrived at his house a couple hours earlier than expected. He was watching a baseball game on TV. The door was unlocked and I let myself in. Steve said 'Hi' and nodded in his minimalist way toward an open chair. I plopped down to watch. When Insoo arrived an hour later, Steve and I were happily engrossed; although I saw no problem, I gathered that Insoo was very concerned that I had not been served drinks and appetisers. When the game was over, Steve cooked the delicious multi-course feast that he had prepared for us and some other guests who arrived at the appointed time.

Steve was brilliantly clear in his thinking, always separating the wheat from the chaff. He had a twinkle in his eye, and usually enjoyed himself. He was a very decent person. He provided intellectual and personal inspiration and support for many of us. I was sitting in the audience in Park City, Utah, at the 2004 Conference on Solution-Focused Practices, when Steve was asked, during a public interview, about important books. I leaned forward to hear his answer, expecting a poststructuralist reading list. I was very touched when, instead, he extolled a recent collection of John and Abigail Adams' correspondence, noting that they began their letters to one another, "Dear Friend".

I last saw Steve at another Erickson conference, December 2004, again in Phoenix. One night we went for a little walk, and wound up at a hamburger joint across from the hotel. He didn't look well, and I had heard that he was having serious health problems. He answered my questions directly. After a bit, we went on to talk about other things. I raised the idea of our doing a joint presentation, possibly another public interview, at the 2005 Solution Focused Brief Therapy conference to be held the next November in Ft. Lauderdale, Florida. Steve demurred: "I may not be there." I didn't get it: "What do you mean, not be there? You're the developer of solution-focused therapy! How can you not be there?" Steve gave a wan half-smile, then shrugged: "Well, you never know for sure, do you?"

We didn't pursue the conference idea but we stayed in touch, occasionally exchanging e-mails, discussing an article, passing on a funny joke. In August 2005, I had been getting ready to go on a big trip to Hong Kong and mainland China, and had written Steve asking for any suggestions. I got back an e-mail – alas, our final communication: "Should be some good eats – have fun!"

A few weeks later, I received from my good friend Harvey Ratner the news of Steve's death in Vienna on September 11, 2005.

I was very saddened by Steve's passing, but nothing could have prepared me for the shock a little over a year later when my computer chimed and I opened an e-mail (I don't recall who sent it) to read: "Insoo Berg died yesterday (January 10, 2007)". I sat in my office stunned, then cried a bit, then walked around my clinic in a daze, then somehow made it through the rest of the day. At home that night, I sent messages to friends. A few days later, as I read the lovely tribute Yvonne Dolan had written, I cried again.

For me, Insoo was always a bright light. We were friends – I used to joke and call her my "Seoul sister". We cheered for one another, and helped one another. We published a chapter together on couple therapy (Hoyt & Berg, 1998), and sometimes I show video clips of her doing therapy as part of my workshop presentations. In my book *Some Stories Are Better than Others*, I wrote:

> More recently, I was viewing a videotape of Insoo Kim Berg [1994] working with a married couple.
>
> On the tape, in her introduction to the session, she commented on the importance of attending to language and the value of using a "not-knowing" posture in which the clients' expertise is especially

respected and supported ... Watching Insoo work, I suddenly had the image of the compassionate Buddha (perhaps prefigured by her Asian countenance), who holds up his palm facing the viewer so as to reflect back whatever is offered ... However, I had the idea that the therapist's hand, rather than simply "reflecting and clarifying" like a flat mirror a la Carl Rogers was a special kind of mirror that could become convex or concave and swivel this way and that – expanding or shrinking the reflected image, opening parts of the story and closing others! Isn't this what (constructive) therapists do?

Questions draw interest here or there, inviting one to focus attention and consciousness in (it may be hoped) helpful ways. [Hoyt, 2000, pp. 66–67]

In my chapter on solution-focused couple therapy for *The Clinical Handbook of Couple Therapy* – which Insoo said was the best she had read – I quoted my then 7-year-old son after he watched part of the same videotape of Insoo working with the couple:

> "Hey, Dad – that's good! Instead of letting them fight, she's getting them to talk about ways they could be happier!" [Hoyt, 2002, p. 360]

I suspect it was Insoo who got me invited to be part of the faculty at the First Pan-Pacific Brief Therapy Conference, held in Fukuoka, Japan, in 1995. Insoo and Steve (and other esteemed American, Canadian, and Japanese colleagues, and my son Alex) were there when I gave the opening keynote speech at the Second Pan-Pacific Brief Therapy Conference, held in Osaka in 2001, and it was Insoo who made arrangements for my son and I to stay at someone's house and have a variety of wonderful cultural experiences. At the end of the conference, I met privately with Insoo (and Mary Goulding) and let them both know of my feelings of eternal respect and appreciation. I still get choked up sometimes when I hike my favourite trail near my home and come to the part I used to imagine someday walking and talking with Insoo. Damn, that ain't gonna happen.

Like many others, I have thought gratefully many times about our contacts and how much Steve and Insoo are woven throughout my world of ideas and relationships.

References

Berg, I. K. (1994). *Irreconcilable Differences: A Solution-Focused Approach to Marital Therapy*. Videotape. Milwaukee: Brief Family Therapy Center.

Hoyt, M. F. (1994). On the importance of keeping it simple and taking the patient seriously: A conversation with Steve de Shazer and John Weakland. In M. F. Hoyt (Ed.), *Constructive Therapies* (pp. 11–40). New York: Guilford Press. Reprinted in M. F. Hoyt (2001). *Interviews with Brief Therapy Experts* (pp. 1–33). Philadelphia: Brunner/Routledge.

Hoyt, M. F. (1996) Solution building and language games: A conversation with Steve de Shazer (and some after words with Insoo Kim Berg). In M. F. Hoyt (Ed.), *Constructive Therapies* (Vol. 2, pp. 60–86). New York: Guilford Press. Reprinted in M. F. Hoyt (2001). *Interviews with Brief Therapy Experts* (pp. 158–183). Philadelphia: Brunner/Routledge.

Hoyt, M. F. (2000). *Some Stories Are Better Than Others*. Philadelphia: Brunner/Routledge.

Hoyt, M. F. (2001). *Interviews with Brief Therapy Experts*. New York: Brunner-Routledge.

Hoyt, M. F. (2002) Solution-focused couple therapy. In A. S. Gurman & N. S. Jacobson (Eds.), *Clinical Handbook of Couple Therapy* (3rd ed., pp. 335–369). New York: Guilford Press. Updated version reprinted in M. F. Hoyt (2009). *Brief Psychotherapies: Principles and Practices* (pp. 139–198). Phoenix, AZ: Zeig, Tucker & Theisen.

Hoyt, M. F., & Berg, I. K. (1998). Solution-focused couple therapy: Helping clients construct self-fulfilling realities. In F. M. Dattilio (Ed.), *Case Studies in Couple and Family Therapy* (pp. 203–232). New York: Guilford Press. Reprinted in M. F. Hoyt (2000). *Some Stories Are Better than Others* (pp. 143–166). Philadelphia: Brunner/Mazel.

Michael F Hoyt Ph.D, Kaiser Permanente Medical Center, Dept. of Psychiatry, San Rafael CA, USA.

Luc Isabaert   Bruges, Belgium

Steve in Bruges

I remember ... Steve and I sitting in the tiny living room at Karthuizerinnenstraat 6, Bruges, my home then in Bruges and Steve's home away from home in Europe, where he used to come when he had a few days free between workshops. We would be sitting there each at one side of the woodstove, reading, for one or two hours, in companionle silence. A whole hour could pass with just four or five phrases exchanged, and these only because we thought them worth saying. That was Steve's ideal of a perfect evening: not one word of small talk, just the warm glow of a coal stove and of friendship ...

I remember ... Steve's long walks through Bruges. Mostly alone and at night. Once he was almost run over, I think it was by a bicycle. The police came and found the tramp they had seen so often, his strangely coloured cloth cap drawn deep over his eyes, glowering at the sidewalk as if he had an argument with it – they had a file on him as an unknown homeless person who would vanish for weeks on end and then suddenly reappear. Now they discovered that this tramp was in fact an American professor who was a guest at the house of a well-known doctor at St. John's hospital ... Well, actually, a psychiatrist ... So maybe ...

I remember ... One night as he was walking, Steve was attacked by three British louts who had come over for a football match and whose idea of a good time was to beat up an elderly man and steal his purse. Only Steve was too fast for them and they only succeeded in breaking his finger. Of all the years I lived in Bruges, this was the only instance I heard of a person being attacked in the streets, and it had to be Steve!

I remember ... One evening, it must have been the eve of an EBTA meeting, because there were eight or ten of us filling up my little living room, Steve had been there for two or three days, Insoo was flying in from Asia, they hadn't seen each other for a few weeks. I had left the street door ajar, and suddenly Insoo stood there. How Steve's eyes lit up! And how Insoo's twinkled! They didn't last long in our company, just long enough for Insoo to say hello to everybody, and off they went to Steve's room. We didn't see them again that evening.

I remember ... The first time we invited Steve. A friend of mine in Paris, Maurice Wajeman, at whose unit I was teaching systemic therapy, had told me I should read *Patterns of Brief Family Therapy* by someone called Steve de Shazer. Maurice said it looked a lot like what I was teaching them. I found he was right, and after reading a few more articles by Steve I decided we must invite him to teach a workshop, as I felt sure we could learn a lot more if we saw and heard him. So I invited him for a workshop in Paris and one in Bruges. This was 1989; he came in 1990. I goofed in the invitation: one of Steve's articles I had read was an early one about the crystal ball technique. I asked him specifically to talk about that. He gently answered that he didn't use that procedure anymore, because he had found it unnecessarily complicated. Of course I didn't know he and Insoo had invented the miracle question by then.

Steve was still rather shy at that time when doing a seminar. In Bruges, I was the only one he knew, from the Paris workshop and from driving from Paris to Bruges in my car. So I was the only person in the audience he looked at from time to time. At one point he had been explaining about his passion for simplicity and for eliminating all hypotheses and techniques that didn't directly contribute to the results. He had me soul-searching already: we did have good results, so obviously we must be doing at least some things right, but perhaps we were too complicated? At that point in my reflections, Steve, who had been looking at the ceiling and over the heads of the participants, suddenly looked right into my eyes and slowly articulated, "Can it be that simple?"

For three weeks, every night I woke up in the middle of the night with those piercing eyes boring into mine and that question: Can it be that simple?

After that, I used to smile inwardly every time someone asked Steve what he thought about hypnosis and he curtly answered, "You don't need it". If ever there was a master at the induction of a naturalistic trance in a client, that man was Steve de Shazer.

I remember … Sometimes Steve had cooked for me when I came back from the hospital in the evening. He did excellent soups, I remember one in particular with grated ginger, chives and some very fresh cod from the fish market two streets away. Or we would cook together; I would start out with a traditional recipe and Steve would suggest an unexpected twist to it. Sometimes it turned out quite nice, sometimes less so. One unhappy experiment was when he mixed blood wurst into sauerkraut. With Polish bigosh I think it would have worked well: it isn't sour at all. With the German- style, very sour sauerkraut we get in Belgium, it was a disaster.

Beer was a frequent topic of conversation. I'm a brewer's son, and Steve loved beer. We agreed that the best lager in the world is Jever, from the eponymous town in the Frisian part of Lower Saxony, Germany. The best beer in the world for him was the Garre Tripel, which you can only drink in the Garre café in Bruges, five minutes from our house. I agreed with him, if only for patriotic reasons. When I was in Milwaukee I tasted the Pilsner- style beer he had brewed himself, and found it "not too bad".

I remember … we seldom talked about therapy. We sometimes discussed cases, but Steve didn't relish conversations about therapeutic topics with other therapists. He seemed to have made up his mind about what was important and that was it. On the other hand, he enjoyed discussing therapy with philosophers like Matthias Varga von Kibéd or anthropologists like Michael Houseman who knew about SFBT and could comment on it from another perspective. We did discuss philoso-phy, and of course in particular Wittgenstein. I had read the Philosophical Investigations and could talk about language games and things like that. But I couldn't make head or tail of most of the Tractatus. Steve obviously could, and he would explain his personal gloss of some item. I'm afraid even so I often remained unenlightened. The impression remains however that in Wittgenstein, Steve always looked beyond the mere logic to the existential implications of yet another obscure phrase.

We also discussed music. We both were fond of Mahler and of Shostakovitch's chamber music. And Steve would explain at length about finger settings on the saxophone or recall anecdotes about his time with Duke Ellington and his musicians.

One point it took me several years to understand was this: I had been doing therapy for twenty years before I met Steve, I had developed procedures and techniques that worked well, so I didn't abandon them, I just added things like the miracle question or scales which we hadn't been using in Bruges before. I would discuss one or other aspect of the Bruges model to check what Steve thought about it and he generally agreed with what I said. Like with Yvonne Dolan however, who also went on inventing techniques for particular clients when the usual ones didn't work, Steve seemed to approve what we did but never took it up to integrate it in his model.

It took me some time to understand that this was how Steve's genius worked: not only eliminate what isn't useful, but even if it is, scrap it if it isn't essential. Yvonne and I are first of all clinicians; Steve was in essence a scientist and a philosopher. The razor Steve wielded was honed even sharper than Ockham's.

One last word perhaps for those who knew Steve only slightly. At times, he could be short-tempered, abrasive, and even disagreeable. Empathy in the sense of suffering in tune with someone else wasn't helpful in his eyes. But he was very concerned and caring with his clients and his friends, and above all, he was wholly and deeply a good man.

Luc Isebaert MD is a physician, trainer and supervisor and a Director of Korzybski International.

Peter De Jong   Grand Rapids, Michigan, USA

My time with Steve and Insoo in Milwaukee

The first I heard of Steve, Insoo, and BFTC was in 1989 after reading a *Family Networker* article describing the "new brief therapies". Steve had written a brief column describing the notion of "exception", which caught my attention. I had just completed a mid-career shift away from teaching and doing research in the sociology of gender roles and deviant behaviour, and was now doing psychotherapy from a psychodynamic perspective. I was listening for and reflecting back the transference I perceived in my clients' actions and language. I had several cases which were not going well, so I decided to try asking exception questions. I discovered, much to my amazement, that practically all of my clients were having successes amid their struggles and the more we talked about these, the more progress they made. So three months later I was in Milwaukee participating in my first workshop at BFTC.

That first workshop in 1990 was easily the most exciting experience of my professional life to that point. Insoo, as usual, ran the workshop doing most of the teaching and then signalling when she wanted someone else to do one of the things on the participants' wish list. So on day two she said, "Steve, you want to talk about theory now, right". Steve grumbled a bit and said, "yes". Then he did something quite remarkable. He set two chairs out facing one another at the front of the room, sat down in one, and then said if anyone had a question during his talk, she or he had to come up and sit in the second chair and ask the question face-to-face with him and he would answer. He then started talking about language and how it works in therapy. Those of us who had questions came up, sat down and asked our questions, and in every case the question served as an opener for a dialogue between Steve and questioner. It was not long before the content of his talk about how language works in therapy was being parallelled in the moment in our workshop interaction.

Other things stirring my imagination in that first workshop were the abundant curiosity, openness to multiple perspectives, and the anticipation of discovery that attended all the conversations. Insoo regularly had a tape recorder operating because she wanted to capture the conversations. With my sociological background in symbolic interactionism I was up in Steve's questioner's chair frequently, dialoguing backing and forth with him. Steve and Insoo were working on their paper, "Doing Therapy: A Post-Structural Re-Vision" (de Shazer and Berg, 1992) and invited me to stay after the workshop to continue talking. So we spent another half day discussing which language might most usefully convey the notion that solutions and client change involve the renegotiation (or deconstruction/reconstruction) of meanings. I came away from that first experience with Steve and Insoo so enthused and flooded with ideas about how to do therapy differently that I was writing notes on a pad of paper perched on a stack of newly-purchased SFBT books sitting on the passenger's seat of my car as I drove through Chicago traffic on my way back to Michigan.

I had the good fortune of returning each summer for 16 years to BFTC to sit in on and participate in workshops with Steve and Insoo, and work on writing and training projects primarily with Insoo. Insoo and Steve always invited workshop participants to their home for "the world's best pizza" the evening of the first day of a workshop. Insoo assigned Steve and me the task of setting up the tables and chairs in the backyard and going out for the pizza and drinks. That gave me several hours to talk with Steve. I learned about his love for the city of Milwaukee and its history, his love/hate relationship with its baseball team the Milwaukee Brewers, brewing beer, and his appreciation of eau-de-vie. I also slipped in some questions about doing therapy. For instance, I once asked, "Steve, when you are interviewing a client, what do you most try to do?" "Absorb," he said emphatically. I responded, "What are you most trying to absorb?" He replied brusquely, "what the client is saying of course." I knew then that the conversation was over; he had said all he wanted or all he wanted me to hear.

My enduring impression of Insoo was her uncompromising passion and energy for spreading SFBT throughout the therapy world wherever there were any who might listen. Her belief in clients' capacities to build a better life by drawing on their potential to envision a "miracle" future and identify related exceptions was unshakable; all that was needed were therapists who knew how to respect the person and the language of clients by asking useful, SFBT-inspired questions. My relationship with Insoo was built on working on ways to make SFBT more accessible to those who wanted to learn it. New and ongoing learners attest that SFBT is "simple but not easy". She and I were in regular contact for 17 years always talking about ways to more clearly convey "how to do SFBT". These conversations led to our joint writings, the videos we planned, and the training projects we shared.

The collaborative work with Insoo was exciting and satisfying and I learned immeasurably from her. She would say, "Peter, be sure to take all the toughest cases you can; you will learn much more about how to do therapy from those than the easy ones". She would say, "Never turn an invitation down to come and teach SFBT; if you do, they will not ask again and we may not ever get another chance to work with them". She was driven by an unwavering wish to be helpful to clients. She had a special place in her heart for women whose children were at risk of being removed for supposed child neglect. I rarely saw her cry, but several times she cried when she heard of cases in our child welfare work in Michigan when a child was removed and the case information indicated the child was removed for marginal neglect, and the worker was completely focused on problem detail to the exclusion of asking about what the mother cared about, her competencies, and her possibilities. Insoo also had an amazing work ethic. I would call her on the first of January to wish her a "happy new year". After thanking me, she would ask me what I was doing and I would say spending the day with family and friends and enjoying myself and she would say with a laugh, "Peter, I knew you were a lazy bum and not working today; me, I cancelled the holidays and am doing something useful".

Insoo and Steve were superb therapists; for me, the best ever. They saw possibilities and resources in the language of clients where others perceived problems and pathology. They spent their careers researching and inventing useful questions and responses that invited clients to build more satisfying lives. Whenever I travel the roads in Michigan and Wisconsin now that I travelled with Insoo and sometimes with Steve, my heart goes heavy and the tears come. I miss them both very much.

Reference

de Shazer, S. and Berg, I. K. (1992). Doing Therapy: A Post-Structural Re-Vision. *Journal of Marital and Family Therapy* 18(1), 71–81.

Peter De Jong, *Ph.D., LMSW* is an emeritus professor of sociology & social work (Calvin College, Michigan, USA) and a former SFBT practitioner in mental health. He co-authored many publications with Insoo Kim Berg including four editions of the book *Interviewing for Solutions* now translated into twelve languages. He currently mentors, trains, and consults with those interested in learning SFBT. He also conducts microanalysis research on therapy conversations with colleagues Janet Bavelas, Harry Korman, and Sara Smock Jordan.

Peter Kaimer   Bamberg, Germany

Markers in rough terrain:
Three memories of Steve and Insoo

It must have been around the year 1984/85. I had been working for six years as a psychotherapist, my outlook coloured by a somewhat pessimistic Austrian soul. I was just starting to apply the ideas about problem-solving in complex systems (Dörner et al., 1983) to the field of psychotherapy (Kaimer, 1986).

At this time, I met Steve and Insoo at a workshop in Vienna. Two statements by Steve, which he presented dogmatically in his quirky, uncompromising style, touched me then and have stayed with me since.

The first reminded me of my philosophical roots, which I had somewhat neglected at the time, because he quoted William of Ockham, whom I revered: "stay simple" and "simplify". Steve thus restored what I had lost: a lasting bridge back to philosophical thought (as he did again later, to Wittgenstein) in the context of psychotherapeutic discourse.

The second statement, arising from his "anti-psychology", was "Look for the exceptions, you fool", and this freed me from the pathological problem-fixation that typified psychotherapeutic diagnosis or case conceptualisation.

In subsequent years, together with my "Bamberger team",[1] which I then headed, I attended two intensive workshops run by Insoo and Steve in Salzburg. And here I want to focus on two experiences that were extremely important for me.

---

[1] The outpatient clinic of the Department of Clinical Psychology / Psychotherapy at the University of Bamberg.

Until then, I had always experienced and associated the embodiment of therapeutic approaches with particular individuals. With Steve and Insoo I now experienced the solution-focused approach in two extremely different personalities who were, however, in all essentials, in total harmony. This allowed me to focus on the quintessence rather than attempting to copy the master's attitude.

The second experience relates to the fact that I had accepted a managerial position at an outpatient's clinic at a relatively earlier stage in my career: shoes which, at the time, were too big for me. My earlier teachers had encouraged me, believed in me – and yet I never had the feeling that they really took me seriously as a person.

At the first workshop in Salzburg, I mustered all my courage and took along a video recording of a therapy session in which I attempted to follow the approach that I had learned in the previous workshop in Vienna and in Steve's book "Patterns of Brief Therapy". The praise and especially the recognition that Steve imparted in his very wise, namely, indirect,[2] manner, touched and encouraged me deeply and lastingly. In the subsequent period, this encouragement continued as Steve acknowledged the role of the "Bamberg team" in the solution-focused scene, occasionally drawing the attention of those working in Milwaukee at the BFTC or attending courses there, to us.

In subsequent years we as a team had the opportunity to conduct supervision workshops with Steve in Nuremberg to discuss our work with him. Here we always got new ideas and confirmation and every day we were able to observe him working with clients when he conducted sessions.

---

[2] One evening at dinner he asked a woman on my team, just loud enough for me to hear, "Are the other team members as good as he is?"

References

Dörner, D., Kreuzig, H. W. & Reither, F. (1983). Lohhausen. Bern: Huber.

Kaimer, P. (1986). Therapie in komplexen Systemen. *Verhaltensmodifikation 7*(4), 213–234.

Peter Kaimer Ph.D., Bamberg, Germany, Department of Clinical Psychology / Psychotherapy at the University of Bamberg. 50% Organisational director of the psychotherapeutic outpatient clinic and 50% psychotherapeutic practice (psychotherapy, educational therapy, supervision).

Esther-Maria Keil
Berlin, Germany

Konstevezius

Like all of you, those catchy categorical imperatives of Steve's therapy have accompanied me throughout my entire career as well as in my personal life. They almost always engender a smile: not only within me, but often in my conversation partners. Nevertheless, it is often simple, if not easy, to follow them.

I had the good fortune to accompany Steve and Insoo on their last professional visits to Berlin and to spend a few evenings with Steve enjoying good Korean or Alsatian cuisine. Since a thorough knowledge of English and philosophy, especially of course that of Wittgenstein, was advantageous, I took my husband with me as a precaution.

Unfortunately, I cannot reconstruct in any detail the firework of insights about history and humanity that took place that evening. I was too fascinated to write anything down, and it required all my abilities just to follow and roughly understand what was said. For days, that evening remained topic number one at home, all the more so as we began to grasp the meaning of Steve's famously pithy statements.

One issue, however, we remember very well. It is a topic which family therapists frequently run up against: how to handle and apply rules. On one of our evenings at Kollwitzplatz however, a slightly different approach to rules was being considered. Namely, that intelligent and forward-looking thinking must (or may) sometimes commit a clear breach of rules in order to bring about substantial progress or benefits for many people. Thus President Thomas Jefferson broke the democratic principles that he had so vehemently pursued when, without obtaining support from his parliament, he accepted Napoleon's offer to sell him the Louisiana territory for $15 million, which Napoleon required to finance his European military campaign. America thus acquired for a pittance its then 18th state, thus doubling in one fell swoop its previous size.

The issues are not always so weighty or costly when we therapists accompany our clients or when parents advise their children. Nevertheless, we are often put in situations that demand all our wisdom. Steve's deep knowledge of the psyche and his incredible ability to get to the heart of the matter in a manner that combines friendly attention and profound humour, to expose something that seems to be a natural given and yet effective, sets a standard which, though hardly attainable, is nevertheless worth trying to emulate.

All this I had already experienced repeatedly when I was able to listen to him for days and experience him in action as a therapist. The most fascinating example for me occurred when, by chance, he was working in the field that defines my daily professional life: the mother of a 14–year boy old diagnosed with ADHD asked how she could still influence her son. Steve's answer was as follows: she should note when her son abided by the rules or would do something desirable, but not let him know that she had noticed this. Rather, she should get a little present for him and give it to him some time later, but by no means should she tell him why she had done this. Just because she felt like it, she should tell him.

Please take time to let the profundity of this intervention and all its aspects sink in! Only when you have fully appreciated it can you – perhaps! – have the same impact by putting together all your documentation on rules for learning, points systems, intermittent reinforcement, and behaviour patterns characterised by hope. Good luck!

I am very grateful to have been allowed to experience at first-hand what an indescribably clever, deeply humorous person, a philanthropist blessed with irony, in a word, a wise man, is. His name is Steve de Shazer.

Esther-Maria Keil is a psychotherapist in private practice in Berlin, Germany. Trainer and supervisor at the North German Institute for Brief Therapy, NIK. Co-author of the therapy concept SMILE for AD(H)S-children and their parents and author of the game *Draw A Square*.

Harry Korman   Malmö, Sweden

Meeting Steve de Shazer and Insoo Kim Berg

I knew Steve de Shazer for almost 20 years and over the course of all these years he only once told me something I was doing wrong and what I might want to do instead. Sometimes I think that I would have learnt solution focused brief therapy quicker if both he and Insoo had not been so solution focused in their teaching but who knows. Anyway . . .

Memory is slippery but I believe we are somewhere in the mid-1990s and Steve is doing a workshop for us in Malmö. As usual he stays with us and the evening after the first day we are sitting in front of the fireplace, having had a good dinner, some wine and we are into our second cognac. It's not easy to converse with Steve, particularly about therapy but I feel a bit more daring than usual and I have had this question on my mind for quite some time. And then I ask it,

"How do you do it?"

He looks questioningly at me and I continue. "Here you are again today, showing another one of those great tapes from BFTC. A tape where your client answers your questions, collaborates with you and works really hard. It's like when I was at BFTC and all the clients there did that and they are not at all like mine who only answer 'I don't know, I don't know'. So did you invent a special detector that you have put at the entrance of BFTC that senses who will answer 'I don't know' and then a trapdoor opens and they are flushed right back out on the parking lot or how do you it?" I notice that I sound almost accusatory and Steve laughs quietly and says,

"Harry. You work too hard."

Solution focused brief therapy is for lazy therapists so I react as if I have just received the ultimate insult.

"What do you mean!!!!?"

"I'll show you", answers Steve and he asks me to put one of my tapes into the video machine.

I put a tape in the player and we look at the beginning of one of my sessions. I see myself starting the session by asking the client, "So what needs to be different as a result of this session for you to be able to say that it was not a waste of your time?"

The client answers, "I don't know" and I immediately ask, "Something small in what you do, feel or think?" and the client answers, "I don't know" and I immediately lean forward and ask, "Perhaps something that someone else might notice?" and the client answers, "I don't know" and then I lean even further forward now trying to formulate the question slightly differently and the client again answers, "I don't know".

Once I am focused on it, it is easy to see that I am working very hard so now Steve picks one of his tapes and puts it in the machine and we look at his opening question. At the time he asked some variation on the same theme as I did: "What needs to happen as a result of you seeing me for you to be able to say that it was worth your time coming in to see me?"

And for the first time over all those years that I had tried to learn solution focused brief therapy I noticed that the client actually answered, "I don't know." A long silence followed and then the client continued, "I don't know – but perhaps I would feel happier". Steve picks up the word 'happier" and asks how other people will notice when the client feels happier and again the client answers, "I don't know". The client thinks for a while and then says, "Perhaps they would notice me joking more" and the session is on its way in the usual way.

Then Steve explains: "Therapeutic conversations follow the same conversational rules as ordinary conversations. It's turn-taking. It's my turn and then it's your turn and then it's my turn again. We take turns and we offer turns. When a question is answered the turn returns to the questioner. Once I have acknowledged or responded to the client's answer it is my turn to continue. If the client says 'I don't know' and I don't take my turn – if I don't do anything – it's still the client's turn and the client will eventually come up with an answer."

We look closely at the tape again.

Steve asks his first question and the client answers, "I don't know". Steve does not respond, he does nothing at all. He just sits there looking at the client waiting. The client looks at him, then looks up to the left, stays like that for a couple of seconds and then his gaze wanders back to Steve and then he says, "I don't know – but perhaps I would feel happier". Steve says, "Okay" and then asks his next question.

Steve explains some more. It sounds as if he's talking about the sociology of language: "In ordinary conversation there is what we used to call the six-second rule. Six seconds is the time it takes for a silence to become awkward. Before that it is just the time it takes for someone to think about an interesting question."

"This is difficult", I say and Steve says, "Yes it is. We are so damned polite and helpful so we tend to nod or say 'uhum' and then we don't get an answer because after that the client expects us to continue."

When I think back to this evening and what Steve taught me that night a story comes to mind. I don't remember if Steve told it or if I read it but it's about the minimalism and the doing as little as possible which he shared with John Weakland.

Steve was married to a Korean woman and John was married to a Chinese woman. The rules of behaviour in their extended families in the Orient are very complex and complicated and if you broke those rules it could happen that you wouldn't be forgiven for several generations. So the only way to not break any of those important rules was to develop huge expertise in doing nothing. So both John and Steve became experts at doing nothing and they came to be seen by their extended families in the Orient as being wise.

Harry Korman MD is a physician in, Malmö, Sweden. Director, manager and supervisor in the SFBT SIKT Malmö, Sweden.

Jan Kuipers   Groningen, Netherlands

Respectful-Patient-Creative-Original-Unique:
Meeting Insoo Kim Berg

A few years ago, I had the honour to be invited (through Coert Visser) to interview Insoo Kim Berg. This interview took place at the trainers' conference "To teach is to learn twice" in Amsterdam. Afterwards, I continued to be in regular contact with her when she returned to the Netherlands to give a training or workshop. In my view, Insoo is very strong in being able to identify the strengths of others in a respectful way. Most of the conversations she leads start by giving acknowledgement and then go directly to asking about the goal that the other person wants to achieve. Her questions quickly help the other person create a perspective of what it is they want.

She is original, patient, curious in the interaction and she knows better than anybody else how to give the "attitude of not-knowing" an organic form. It is wonderful to see how she is able to reframe the client's reaction or how she can elicit constructive formulations while simultaneously giving recognition to the problems expressed by the client. For example, when a client says that she is afraid, Insoo would reframe it by saying, "Oh, you know when it feels safe or unsafe". In my perception, this reframing or reframe is a great opportunity to identify strengths in others. Insoo gives creative feedback which gives the client room and which is respectful. Often, the client is pleasantly surprised by Insoo's reframing.

I keep remembering one fascinating and unforgettable moment when Insoo was talking with a female client who apparently wanted nothing. A few psychologists were sitting in an adjacent room and were following the conversation via a one-way mirror. Insoo asked her what the purpose of her visit was. The client reacted to this first question of Insoo's with a rather dismissive glance and turned her head away.

Insoo kept sitting quietly, waited a while and asked a question along the lines of, "What would you like to see happening?" The client responded by looking down and turning away from Insoo. Insoo got up, took a piece of A4 paper and started writing on it. The client turned her head a little bit in the direction of Insoo, apparently hearing the sound of writing on the paper.

Insoo put the paper on her lap and sat back down in her seat. She had written: "I am impressed with your tenacity". The client grabbed the paper, tore it in half and threw it on the ground.

After some silence, Insoo got up again and walked to a blackboard with some chalk. She wrote in large letters: "I am impressed with your energy!" The client looked in the direction of the board and of Insoo. Insoo was smiling. In that moment a hesitant laugh broke out in the client. Insoo went and sat down next to her asking, "Did you know that? Did you know that?" The client reacted with a somewhat embarrassed laugh saying, "No ...".

The question that Insoo asked after this was: "How would you like to leave this room soon?" The woman reacted: "Happy". Insoo then asked the question: "What needs to happen now, so that you will soon leave and be happy again?" The client hesitated, shrugged her shoulders but then said the following: "That I can notice again that I get energy from my work".

Insoo: "Mmm, this is interesting ... if I ask you on a scale of 1 to 10, where 10 stands for you having enough energy and 1 stands for the opposite. Where are you at this moment?"

Client: "Ee ... I am at about 3."

Insoo: "How do you manage to keep it up?"

A small tear ran across the face of the client and Insoo waited patiently until a small smile appeared.

Insoo: "Imagine that one day you are at a 10, what would it look like when you are at a 10?"

Then the client gently started to talk about little things that would be different. Insoo continued with the well-known question: "What else?"

A large number of small changes were mentioned. The client got into a sort of flow and then Insoo asked how her colleagues would notice. This last question was a sort of turning point leading to a mental shift in the client.

In total, the session lasted a bit over half an hour, after which Insoo took a break and asked us, "What impressed you about what the client said or did?" Insoo then passed on the feedback we had given as constructive feedback to the client. The guiding idea behind this is:

What you pay attention to, grows.

This feedback from Insoo did not take long and she mentioned the commitment and the persistence of the client. To round off the feedback, she acknowledged that the client had a very clear picture of what 10 looked like. Then she asked the question of what it would look like if the client moved up from a 3 to a 4: "What is different then?" The client was able to identify clearly what would be different and ended by saying, "I did not expect that it would be so fast and I am very relieved and happy."

In short: **Less can be a lot** . . . Stay respectful and on the surface with questions . . . it may be simple, but it is not easy.

Thanks to Insoo, who gave me a framework of thinking through which I am able to spread these ideas. I will always think about these following unique statements of Insoo and Steve:

- If you want to go fast . . . go slow
- Leading from one step behind.

Jan Kuipers Drs is a GZ Psychologist (NVO) and Supervisor in Postgradute Orthopedagogiek Studies of the Groningen (UPO-G). He is mainly active in education as a senior consultant, and is the owner of On Wings of Solutions, Assen, the Netherlands.

Jacek Lelonkiewizc   Łódź, Poland

Miracles, earthquakes and lessons

The first time I met Insoo it was in Jyväskylä, Finland. Or rather I should say I met her for the first time when I came across an announcement for the International Association of Family Therapy's conference there. It was in 1990, and I had just regained my passport and my freedom. Communism had just collapsed.

I had lived the previous eight years of my adult life hearing the words of a security police officer who sentenced me to spend the rest of my time inside the borders of Poland, considered as politically insecure because of my involvement in Solidarity. Being able to have a passport back home was an indescribable experience. It was my miracle number one.

The world had opened to me and I was able to do something remarkable. To watch the world. To learn something new. But in moments like this, when one can do anything – one often acts blindly, frozen in fear. I hoped I would act wisely.

By complete chance I found the announcement of the Jyväskylä conference and saw a post-conference workshop on working with alcohol-dependent people without resistance. Such an idea was a total heresy for me, but on the other hand it was quite an alluring idea. So finally I decided to take the plunge. And this was earthquake number one.

I actually went there just to meet Insoo. I was lucky enough to find her there – and I immediately realised what an unusual person she was. She was totally different from other important and famous therapy gurus who walked the conference corridors. She welcomed me in a very warm manner, ready to talk with someone from nowhere. That was my miracle number two.

She invited me to attend her workshop, but with just US$100 in my wallet I wasn`t able to stay there for even a day longer. However after the conference, she answered my letter and started a correspondence with me, sending advice and articles. This was help not to be overestimated – I started to learn Solution Focused practice and soon made a change in my own practice. This was the next earthquake – both in my thinking about therapy and my practice.

Soon Insoo and Steve came to Poland – and this was the next miracle – they came to conduct a workshop at a small conference we organised and we were able to spend some time together. That was the first time I met Steve. I had never met a therapist working in such a manner. He broke all my deep convictions about how therapists ought to behave. With his interrupting when the client was speaking, staring into space or onto the floor, remaining silent for long minutes, he seemed to ignore some parts of what the clients had said. But in spite of these obvious professional mistakes – at least I had been taught to see them as mistakes – clients seemed to be satisfied with the contact and benefited from it! These lessons on therapeutic contact that I got from Steve were truly unforgettable.

When I met Steve and Insoo in private, I had an impression that Steve was somehow hidden in Insoo`s shadow, although it was clear how much they loved and appreciated each other. They visited us in Poland several times, and in 1994 they invited me to come for a summer training in Milwaukee (where I met unusual people like Therese Steiner, Plamen Panayotov and Christina Saunders).

Insoo and Steve were totally different from each other and at the same time they complemented each other. She seemed to be direct, open and clearly interested in other people. She seemed to take care of people and tried to help them. Steve was a taciturn backed-off guy, who surprised everybody with unexpected speeches from time to time. She seemed to be happy to answer questions with a laudably unshake-able patience – he was straight and sharp in his answers, but only if he wanted to answer – usually the question had to be interesting enough. In Milwaukee I spent hours watching as they worked with clients and us – the students of the Brief Family Therapy Center. I benefited from that a lot, as well as from everyday contact with Steve and Insoo. They were both remarkably hard workers. I remember going to BFTC with Insoo on Saturdays and Sundays – but on Sundays only until 3 pm, because they were Sundays. She worked on papers, articles, research. I learned there what hard work means but on the other hand how much fun one can have from work, as long as one is passionate about it. You could see how energetic and full of passion she was by watching her walks on Sunday mornings – long and fast. The atmosphere in the BFTC team was simply wonderful. I got a whole lot of support, from Gale Miller as well – my cordial gratitude goes also to him.

In Milwaukee for the first time in my life I saw a one-way mirror, recording sessions and preparing copies of them for teaching, and making scripts of the sessions for further analysis as well. Such a systematised work environment was an absolute novelty for me.

I learned there that Steve had his "human face" – he was a very good cook, and that helped me to get closer to him. I saw him smiling, making jokes, drinking beer. I appreciated his wisdom and knowledge as a therapist, incredibly efficient in his interventions, a brilliant teacher and thinker in his sharp and clear responses to our questions.

I also remember Steve and Insoo in London, where I went for a workshop presented by them and Gianfranco Cecchin. A whole room packed with people, half of them interested in SFT, half in systemic work. Steve's answers were sharp, sometimes even ugly, but hitting the meaning precisely. Insoo's remarks were polite, clear and friendly. I was taken by the way Steve and Insoo cooperated with each other, while doing things in a completely different way.

We met several times, here in Poland as well. We spent time both professionally and privately. I have benefited from both. SFBT changed a lot in my private life. New habits helped me to survive difficult times in my life, by looking for what helped and repeating this, no matter how difficult it was. Being focused on doing, versus feeling, helped me to go forward, no matter what the circumstances were.

What lessons have I learned from Insoo and Steve? Here are some of many:

- The client's point of view is the only important one, no matter how outstanding the therapist is.
- I have learned to appreciate the power of small steps towards progress.
- I have learned how important it is to make a well-established goal.
- I gained freedom from taking too much responsibility as a professional.
- I have learned the value of humility.
- I have learned the pleasure of hard work.
- I have learned the value of curiosity.
- I have learned the value of kindness.
- I had to think over my relations with people.
- I have learned to take responsibility for my professional actions – before that I clearly did not understood what that meant.
- I understood the benefits of well-organised work.
- I gained hunger for knowledge and progress in my professional and private skills.
- I have learned to be demanding of myself and not to expect too much from the client.
- I have learned the pleasure of living life intensively.
- I have learned to look for meaning in life.
- I have learned there are no losses when one can learn lessons from failures.

I thank the Lord – or fate – that I came to Jyväskylä. It started a revolution – a set of miracles and earthquakes in my life.

Jacek Lelonkiewicz is a psychotherapist and brief therapist in Łódź, Poland. He is a trainer and supervisor at the Centre for Brief Therapy, Łódź.

Eve Lipchik   Milwaukee, USA

Memories

From 1978 until 1988, I worked closely with Insoo or Steve, or both of them, five days a week. It is, therefore, difficult to isolate a particular memory about them that stands out in my mind as more special, or more characteristic of them. I have therefore decided that the best thing I can do is to "free associate" about the years during which I was closely associated with them.

My first experience with Insoo: she was my supervisor at the Family Therapy Training Institute at Family Service of Milwaukee and she asked me what I would like to know at the end of my Family Therapy training that didn't know then. I said that I believed that I had the unrealistic expectation that after I graduated I would never again have to sit in a session and wonder what to do, or say next. She said that was easy to accomplish and she was right. Commitment to, and understanding of, systemic principles made that wish come true.

My first contacts with Steve: I noticed him at staff meetings at Family Service during my training and asked who the silent man with the dark expressive eyes was. This was a stark contrast to the man I met a few months later in his own home where he and Insoo had therapy sessions with volunteers for experimental purposes. On his own territory that man spoke out clearly and with strong convictions.

Steve was a renaissance man: he knew his classical music; he had played jazz saxophone; he could cook great Chinese food; he made wonderful beer; and had a Jesuit education that afforded him great knowledge of philosophy and classical languages.

Insoo was multi-talented as well. She was a very creative person who could eat a steak and kidney pie in England and come home and reproduce it perfectly without a recipe. Her garden was large and bountiful, and she could sew anything she set her mind to without a pattern.

One autumn Insoo, Steve and I went to an AAMFT meeting in Dallas and the three of us ended up taking a long walk. We were talking about presentation styles and Insoo, always anxious to promote Steve so the world could see what she appreciated in him, urged Steve to project more when he presents. "You should look at the audience more directly!" she said emphatically. Steve mumbled something in reply. Steve had a way of replying at times but really not saying anything clearly when he didn't want to reply. I said, "Well, it's not easy for Steve because he's so shy." Insoo stopped dead in her tracks and said, "Steve is shy?" Then she looked up to him and said, "Steve, are you shy?" and Steve mumbled (if I remember correctly), "Always have been". What a lesson about the eyes of a beloved!

Steve's shyness was reinforced for me one night when we shared a cab to a hotel on the way to a meeting in San Francisco. By that time I must have been working with Insoo and Steve for at least five years. We spent a lot of time together either behind the mirror or sitting around and talking about cases. Some of us would throw in some personal stories occasionally, but Steve never shared anything about his youth or his family's past or present. It was late at night and very dark in the cab and Steve spontaneously began to talk about his past. I sat in silence, amazed that this cover of darkness allowed these revelations.

Insoo got a great deal of satisfaction from mentoring people and helping them reach their potential. I was one of them. I hated speaking in public and as BFTC began to acquire a national reputation, Insoo realised that we all needed to know how to speak publicly about what we were developing at BFTC. Her way of helping me get my feet wet was to start taking me along to her presentations. She insisted that I present a small portion of them. The first time I did a whole presentation by myself she got my husband to go with her and sit in the back row of the auditorium and watch. I think she thought this would be supportive, but it actually made me more nervous. The end result proved to be good, since the praise they showered on me helped me cross what I thought would be an insurmountable barrier.

Steve's way of writing was to take a walk outdoors to compose his thoughts. We all suspected that he also smoked a cigarette or two while walking and thinking since our office was smoke free. Steve's office was across a narrow corridor from mine, and when the doors were open, which was always, we were only about six feet apart. Our desks pointed in the same direction and when Steve was writing "Keys to Solutions" he would pass whatever he had just typed across to me without a word. It was understood that he wanted me to read it and make comments as soon as I could. This silent partnership was very valuable to me and hopefully to him.

Insoo took care of herself by going to the gym regularly and swimming and exercising. After her routine, she would go to the sauna. She would often sit on the floor behind the mirror and stretch while she was listening to a case. One day, during an uneventful moment in a case we were observing, she volunteered that she had fallen asleep in the sauna the night before. If the staff had not checked the sauna before they locked up she could have ended up there all night. We chided her thoroughly and begged her to avoid such a dangerous situation in the future. Others have mentioned that this was not the only incident of this kind. When I read about her untimely death in the sauna at her gym I recalled our warnings, and it reminded me that Insoo was a very strong, determined woman who did not let anything stop her from doing what she set her mind to.

It is difficult for me to adjust to the idea that both Insoo and Steve are gone. Now Elam Nunnally and Jim Derks, the other two people who were in our core group regularly, are gone as well. Only Marilyn LaCourt and I are left. When she and I meet we often talk about how exciting those early days at the Brief Family Therapy Center were. For me, the synergy of the group was one of the most exciting, mind-expanding times in my life. Little did we know that our fantasies about future success would become reality.

Eve Lipchik works in private practice in Milwaukee, Wisconsin, USA. She is founder and owner of ICF Consultants Inc., and is an international trainer and supervisor.

Kurt Ludewig   Münster, Germany

The return to useful practice – or 'What I owe Steve, among other things'

In 1983, at my former workplace, the Department of Paediatric and Adolescent Psychiatry at the Hamburg-Eppendorf University Hospital, we had already gone beyond the Milan approach which we had started to use in 1978. We had distanced ourselves from the overly pragmatic interventions of the Milan style and now enthusiastically rode the aesthetic wave that had emerged in the early 1980s. That was very "pretty", but whether it was useful, we had ceased to ask. At that time, an employee of the BFTC, the educational professor Alex Molnar and his wife, Barbara Lindquist, were embarking on an exchange year in Germany and were using the opportunity to visit Jürgen Hargens in North Germany. We took the opportunity to invite the Molnars for a working visit to our clinic.

They were to conduct a morning session with one of our client families, and in the afternoon we would demonstrate our approach. At that time we required roughly three to four hours per session and we assumed that they would also need that long. Alex led the conversation but after only about 30 minutes he withdrew to consult. He and Barbara put together a concluding intervention in around five minutes, and five minutes later it was all over. They needed less than 40 minutes for something that we usually needed several hours to achieve. We were so amazed and impressed that we could only conduct our afternoon session with difficulty and blushing faces. For me it was clear that I had to learn the source of their approach. So I made use of my participation at a meeting of epistemologists and family therapists in Calgary, organised by Karl Thomm, which represented a considerable financial investment for me, and followed it with a visit to the BFTC in Milwaukee. That was in April 1984.

Once in Milwaukee, I was driven to the Brief Family Therapy Center, where I was warmly received, but with an equanimity that typifies those who frequently welcome visitors. I knew no one there personally as Alex was still in Germany. Without further ado, I was invited to sit behind the one-way mirror and watch Steve work with an Afro-American family. I must confess that despite my reasonable knowledge of English – I had lived and worked for two years in the USA – I understood precious little of the conversation. I focused on Steve and his actions, and concluded that he was just as grumpy and inscrutable in his dealings with his clients as he had been earlier with me. However, the clients seemed to experience Steve differently, because they responded to him in an animated fashion. I was amazed because, of the many qualities which are commonly attributed to psychotherapists, I could discover few of them in Steve. After 30 or 40 minutes he came out, sat down with the observers and asked me what kind of intervention I would adopt for these clients. I came up with a response to which he listened in an indifferent manner, only to say that he would use the Formula First Session Task. He explained that the BFTC team was in the process of testing this standard intervention and would therefore conclude all first sessions in this manner for the coming year.

For someone like me, who was slowly freeing himself from the traditional understanding of psychotherapy in search of a practice that was compatible with the requirements of systemic theory, the first impression in Milwaukee was more confusing than enlightening. It seemed very minimalist and North American, a bit like fast food therapy. But I had the good fortune to be invited to stay with one of the BFTC associates, the Vienna-born Eve Lipchik. In the following evenings, conversing with her and her charming husband Elliot, I had ample opportunity to talk about my experiences in BFTC with this European-influenced couple and slowly bring things into balance.

One evening there was a small reception at Steve's house. Insoo, whom I couldn't relate to especially well, was, if memory serves me, out of town at the time. On this occasion, I experienced Steve in a way that reconciled me to the man whom I had previously known as grumpy and unapproachable. Like many others from Milwaukee, Steve brewed beer. This man who tended to speak sparingly, saying only the bare essentials, suddenly became talkative, even funny. It was an enjoyable evening; I began to get to know Steve as a person.

As far back as November 1985, Steve organised a workshop together with Insoo in our Institute for Systemic Studies, set up in 1984 in Hamburg. He was our first therapeutic guest – besides Maturana and Varela. To my knowledge, we were the first to invite him to Germany. In the meantime, I had studied his books and essays, and I had begun to recognise the value and importance of Steve's brief therapy approach, which he later developed in a solution-focused direction, and I began to integrate it into the way I worked. Without intending to, whenever and wherever I had the opportunity, I became an advocate and populariser of these ideas in the German-speaking world. It thus turned out that Steve became a regular co-worker in Bremen, Vienna and elsewhere. Here in Hamburg, he led workshops about every two years well into the 1990s. On a personal level, we met more often at conferences and other events; we got on well and always had something to tell each other.

I would like to conclude my memories of this great man with two small anecdotes. The first situation arose at the last workshop held in Hamburg. I was able to attend the workshop since I was now living in Münster, having been obliged to leave my previous workplace following a change in the management. Steve had spent the first 90 minutes of the seminar providing a theoretical discourse on the basis of his practices. I considered this to be largely superfluous, since we already possessed a respectable body of theory, especially in Hamburg. I was more interested in his practices and the many innovations he had introduced. In the first break, I told him this as diplomatically as I could. Then something happened which I did not expect at all: he reacted with great offence, saying that in the United States he was being attacked as a European theorist, and I just wanted to hear about his practices. For the rest of the first day, half a morning, and all afternoon, he sat down and showed one video after the other, without much explanation. Only on the second day had he calmed down again.

The second anecdote relates to a dinner held for participants in a seminar at the University of Münster. In stark contrast to his usual behaviour over many years on similar occasions, Steve was jovial, funny, talkative, and this before he had had his first beer. In a quiet moment I asked him privately, how he could account for this diametrical change. He said with full conviction that Insoo had made him aware that he should do more to promote himself during his travels, to be less cautious and to be a little more entertaining. And in this he succeeded marvellously.

The news of his sudden and tragic death touched us all very much. We have lost a great man ... and a good friend.

Kurt Ludewig Dr. phil. is a psychologist, in Münster, Germany. He is an instructing therapist for systemic therapy and counselling (Systemic Society, SG), has 30-year tenure in the Departments of Psychiatry and Psychotherapy, for Children and Adolescents at the universities of Hamburg and Münster, and gives teaching and supervision at the Rhur Institute and at other institutes.

Alasdair J Macdonald   Carlisle, UK

Meeting Steve and Insoo

Most of my memories of Steve and Insoo come from meetings at European Brief Therapy Association (EBTA) conferences and workshops. Steve and Insoo loved Bruges in Belgium and we met one another there on several occasions. Because of his interest in beer and cookery, Steve found Belgium particularly attractive. He claimed that because he was never at home in Milwaukee, he had few friends there. Thus he used to say that he could not stop teaching because all his friends were in other countries.

The EBTA Board meets in Bruges once a year to plan conferences and to have a masterclass in current developments. In one of the earliest of these meetings (1998 or 1999) we had a very memorable evening together. Insoo was teaching elsewhere but Steve and other old friends of his were present.

On the evening before the meeting, we dined in Luc Isebaert's rented house in the old part of the town. The house was a lovely medieval structure on four stories. It had a tiny kitchen and a tiny patch of open ground at the back. Because of some domestic rearrangements, there was a fine grand piano in the sitting room, with the dining table pushed into one corner. So several of us ate standing, with our plates on the top of the piano.

On the journey to Bruges I had read in a magazine about a master chef's favourite Belgian meal: sorrel soup with salmon rillettes on toast, rabbit in a chervil cream sauce and a curd tart for dessert. To my astonishment, Luc provided exactly this menu for all fourteen of us in his tiny kitchen. Of course, Luc has been a restaurateur as well as a psychiatrist. (He also speaks six languages fluently and reads Portuguese and Latin as well, having books in all these languages in his home.) There was no refrigerator in the house. However, the cellar was at the level of the nearby canal and was quite cool. Luc told us that he placed items for storage on the appropriate step of the cellar stairs according to the cooling required!

Many of us had brought a contribution for the meal. However, because of air travel restrictions, most of us had chosen to bring cheese. Luc impressed us after dinner by identifying some twenty different cheeses by scent alone.

After dinner we talked with Steve about many aspects of therapy and its development. Two people played pieces on the grand piano. We asked Steve about his earlier life as a saxophone player in a jazz band. He pointed to the similarity between musicians and therapists. A musician may appear to sit for long periods without activity. Then he plays his notes perfectly in time with the orchestra, then he sits still again. Steve suggested that a therapist may appear inactive, but is actually waiting for his cue and the perfect moment to act. He told us that he never played music now, saying that once you have been a professional in anything, you no longer have an interest in doing it as a hobby or for the entertainment of others. This was a convincing statement to me.

As was his custom during his travels, Steve put on his long coat and his shapeless tweed cap and went out for a walk by himself later in the evening. He would do this even in unfamiliar cities. He said that he would always find himself in somewhere recognisable if he walked for long enough. He had taken such walks alone and with Insoo in Bruges on every visit for many years. We continued to talk around the piano.

Two hours later Steve returned. He told us that he had been knocked down in the street outside by a careless motorcyclist. Luckily he was not hurt. Passers-by had helped him to his feet and a policeman had come to the scene. Steve said to the policeman, 'I am an American therapist staying in Kartuizerinnenstraat'. The policeman replied, 'No, you are not! I have seen you walking about this city at night for many years. You are a Belgian wanderer, not an American!' Eventually the policeman was convinced and allowed Steve to return to the house!

In later years, when Steve became ill, he and I would sometimes correspond by email about his activities at home while Insoo was travelling. He cheerfully criticised his doctors. He spoke of his pleasure in driving his BMW X3 sports car through the meadows of spring flowers and of preparing Korean and Chinese food for his close companions. I was at one of his workshops in London two days before his death. He gave me his ticket for a Bruckner symphony in London because he wanted to rest in the evening. After presenting the next day, he went on to Vienna but became seriously ill on the journey.

After Steve's death, Insoo and I were working on a book of research into solution-focused therapy as a memorial to Steve. We had been speaking about the details of this project the day before her unexpected death in 2007. Others have now taken on the idea and the book has emerged (Franklin, Trepper, McCollum, & Gingerich, 2011) as a memorial to both Steve and Insoo.

I often think of Steve and his dramatic effect on my life, in spite of his dry quiet manner. I always picture him in his long coat, walking through the streets of foreign cities. I would like to think that he may still be out there somewhere, thinking of new ideas as he used to. I guess that Insoo is walking with him, hand in hand as they always were.

Reference

Franklin, C., Trepper, T. S., McCollum, E. E., & Gingerich, W. J. (2011). *Solution-focused brief therapy: A handbook of evidence-based practice.* Oxford: Oxford University Press.

Dr Alasdair J Macdonald is a consultant psychiatrist and family therapist, and research coordinator for the European Brief Therapy Association.

Mark McKergow   London, UK

Steve de Shazer: A different kind of cleverness (... and Paul Gonsalves)

I first met Steve in 1994 at the Interactional View conference in Palo Alto, California. Although I did not know it at the time, this was a milestone event in the development of interactional and systemic ideas – one of the few times where the Mental Research Institute group (Paul Watzlawick, John Weakland and Dick Fisch amongst them) came together with the Solution Focused therapy crowd led by Steve de Shazer and Insoo Kim Berg.

Steve and Insoo had been at MRI two decades earlier, and had introduced new subtleties and simplicity into the MRI model – improvements, as they saw it. However, the link between the two centres was maintained by Steve's relationship with John Weakland, his supervisor and mentor. During a panel discussion Insoo and Paul Watzlawick embraced the view that the two approaches were very similar, while Steve and Dick Fisch thought they were very different.

I next met Steve in London. My colleague Harry Norman had approached him for an interview, which we finally managed to do in London in 1995 (Norman, McKergow & Clarke, 1997). I only discovered later that he was noted for not giving interviews, and that this was a great privilege. Steve was a keen brewer and beer drinker, and Harry had managed to interest him in sampling some "medieval beer", brewed in tiny quantities to authentic recipes. This may have been the key to our success!

In the week before the interview Steve was leading a training in SFBT with a large audience (well over 100 people). Steve ambled onto the stage with a microphone, exhaled deeply as he always did before starting, and said, "So ... you'd better ask me some questions". A shiver went around the room. Surely he was the expert, and we wanted to be told what to do. Yet here he was, refusing to tell us. There was a silence.

"Does it work with alcoholics?", came a question from the floor. "I don't know. Next question." "Does it work with personality disorders?" "I don't know. Next question." Several more diagnoses were mentioned, and each time the answer was the same – "I don't know".

I was amazed and disturbed. Here I was, keen to find out more about this fantastic approach to change, and the star performer was telling me he didn't know if it worked with alcoholics. What was going on? My discomfort was clearly shared by other audience members – after a while, some started to leave.

"Can I see you ask the miracle question?" asked someone. Steve brightened up visibly. "Ah! Yes, I'm sure I can do that. Thanks for asking." We relaxed a little – at least he was going to do *something*.

As the session went on, I reflected on Steve's remarks of "I don't know". Surely this approach did work with many kinds of patient? Were there not studies to prove it? I came to realise that Steve, of course, knew all this perfectly well. Actually, he was showing us how to do Solution Focused therapy in that moment, engaging what I have to come call his 'different kind of cleverness'. In order to answer the apparently simple question "Does it work with alcoholics?", one must accept two presuppositions. Firstly, there is such a thing as an alcoholic. And secondly, that it (the treatment in question) is replicable by anyone who applies it.

Let's look at the first one first – is there such a thing as an alcoholic? Clearly the word is used as if there were, but SF work is not based on diagnosis – the client's complaint is not relevant in determining what they want (the 'solution' in solution-focused terminology) and times when what they want happens already. Steve's work was part of the tradition that questions the value of diagnosis in any case, and even if an accurate assessment of the condition could be made, each client would want something different – leading to a course for treatment which would vary in each case. There was therefore no value in even considering whether the client was an 'alcoholic' or not. Part of his 'I don't know' was a rejection of this as a relevant term in his work.

The other presupposition is in the "Does it work?" element. "Does it work?" implies that "it" is working, rather than someone is acting skilfully to make something happen. We might say of a piano, "Does it work?" – meaning that if someone hits the notes, then the relevant sounds will emerge. It doesn't matter who is hitting the notes, the sounds will emerge. In SFBT, solutions are constructed in conversation, which is an art as well as a science. To ask if SF therapy works is therefore to ask not if the piano works, but instead to ask if piano-playing "works". This is not a sensible question – pianos can be made to sound beautiful with skill, but someone without the skill could scarcely claim that the piano didn't work – just that they were not yet individually skilful enough.

A question which may have had a better reaction from Steve is "Have you had successful outcomes with clients who want to drink less?" In this case, the question is about his own experience, and related to a client group defined in terms of what they wanted. The distinctions between this and "Does it work with alcoholics?" are, for me, at the heart of SF practice. Maybe Steve's legacy to us is to stop trying to answer big questions and focus instead on the tiny micro-construction of conversations which build solutions.

One other occasion springs to mind, when Steve recounted an event from his distant past which I have not seen recorded anywhere else. I was sitting opposite him at a dinner in Malmö and decided to see if I could out-silence him. It worked – he became really quite talkative. In particular he told of a time many years before when he was walking through New York carrying his tenor saxophone. He bustled around the corner and – wham! – bumped into another tenor saxophone-toting gentleman. Steve's instrument was unharmed but the other fellow's sax came out of its case and lay on the pavement, broken, prompting a cry of "Oh no! Duke'll kill me!" "Duke" was Duke Ellington, and the now hornless musician was none other than Paul Gonsalves, the Ellington orchestra's star tenor sax soloist who gained immortality by playing 27 choruses of "Diminuendo and Crescendo in Blue" while the crowd went berserk at the 1957 Newport Jazz Festival.

Gonsalves was on his way to a rehearsal with the Ellington band, and was now short of an instrument. Steve offered his as a temporary replacement, Gonslaves accepted and they went together to the rehearsal where Steve sat and listened. I understand that he subsequently stood in at rehearsals for star musicians who were away. Steve was keen on the "new thing" modern jazz of the 1960s – he told me he had a lot of time for the music of Archie Shepp (also a tenor saxophonist). While many people talk of his love of Shostakovich, I like to remember Steve as a closet jazzer – an improviser both on the bandstand and in the therapy room.

Reference

Norman. H., McKergow, M. & Clarke, J. (1997). Paradox is a muddle: An interview with Steve de Shazer. *Rapport* 34, 41–49. Retrieved from http://sfwork.com/paradox-is-a-muddle.

Mark McKergow PhD, MBA is a partner (with Jenny Clarke) at the Centre for Solutions Focus at Work in London, England. He is co-author and editor of several books about using SFBT ideas, in management and coaching, helped to found the SOLWorld and SFCT communities and edits the SFCT journal *Inter*Action. He is also a visiting research fellow in philosophy of psychology at the University of Hertfordshire.

Gale Miller   Milwaukee, USA

A guy from Milwaukee:
Remembering Steve de Shazer

I first met Steve de Shazer and the rest of the solution-focused brief therapy pioneers in the winter of 1984. We met to discuss what the therapists at BFTC did and whether their work might become a research project for me. Most people would say that the meeting was a success, since I did end up doing the research project that we discussed. I was involved (off and on) with this group and other therapists for more than 20 years. I came to know Steve much better than the others. I will limit my remarks to Steve.

Some of my first impressions of Steve never changed, although they evolved a little bit over time. Most important was my sense of Steve as a guy from Milwaukee. For me, his demeanour represented an old Milwaukee style that was slowly dying when my wife and I moved here in 1976. I don't think Steve would be troubled by my characterisation of him. He embraced his Milwaukee heritage, despite living a life of international travel and influence. For Steve, being a guy from Milwaukee was "not so bad". Steve and I became friends, in part, because we both appreciated the many characters living in our city.

Steve could be gruff and stubborn, but he was not nearly as impatient with others as some other characters from Milwaukee that I have known. I am thinking of Emil, the man who owned the hardware store in my neighbourhood for many years. Both Emil and Steve set some seemingly rigid rules for others. But both were also known to modify or even ignore their rules under the right circumstances. I came to learn that "no" from either one of them often meant "maybe". Similarly, Steve and Emil thought about the next generation. Emil brought his niece into his business and she eventually took it on as her own. Steve spent much of his adult life training others to take his place within the solution-focused brief therapy world. Both achieved these ends while remaining gruff and stubborn to their dying days.

Two rather different Milwaukee influences on Steve were the Jesuit priests at Marquette University High School (MUHS) and Warren Spahn, a pitcher for the Milwaukee Braves baseball team in the 1950s and 1960s. Both the priests and Spahn represented excellence to Steve. He talked often of the rigorous classical education that he received at MUHS and the demanding presence of several priests that he could name and describe decades after graduating. He took pride in both the knowledge and discipline that they taught him. Spahn was one of the greatest pitchers in the history of baseball and probably Steve's favourite baseball player. He always smiled when he talked about watching Spahn pitch. Spahn did not look like an athlete nor did he intimidate batters by throwing blazing fastballs. What Spahn did, however, was to win baseball games for 21 years. He ranks as the sixth winningest pitcher in the history of the game. While different in so many ways, Warren Spahn and his Jesuit teachers were enduring role models for Steve.

The person that Steve talked about the most was his father. So many of Steve's interests were related to his father, who also loved baseball and who relaxed by driving through the Wisconsin countryside. Steve loved to drive and he sometimes pointed out significant places from his youth as he cruised through the city. I remember the day that we passed a restaurant in the centre of the city. Steve casually said, "I took my first girlfriend there on our first date". Steve also told stories of his father's skill as an electrician. In the early years of our acquaintance, Steve emphasised how his father insisted that all electrical problems could be solved in multiple ways. He explained that his father regularly rewired troublesome electrical devices to make certain that if one source of power leading to the devices failed, there was a second source of power already connected to them. In the early years, Steve talked about the relevance of his father's work for therapists in workshops and seminars. I never understood why he stopped talking about it in later years.

Of course, this is a partial list of Milwaukee influences on Steve. My understanding is that his mother – whom he felt great affection for –

was highly significant in fostering his musical interests. She and the other characters I have mentioned here give us some sense of why I continue to remember Steve as a guy from Milwaukee who also happened to do some other things in life. Steve sometimes said that his skills as a therapist were evidence that he stood on the shoulders of the giants who trained him. But, like the rest of us, he also stood on the shoulders of the less celebrated giants who shaped his outlook and character well before he ever encountered the world of therapy.

Gale Miller is a research professor at Marquette University, Milwaukee, USA. Research and numerous publications on Solution-Focused Brief Therapy. International speaker and trainer.

Scott D Miller   Chicago, USA

Harumph and Hard Work: Five Years with Steve de Shazer and Insoo Berg at the BFTC

In late 1987, I sent a letter to Insoo Berg. It was not my first. I had been pouring over the publications coming out of the Brief Family Therapy Center (BFTC) for a couple of years by that time. We had even met briefly at a workshop she taught in a city near my home. Every so often, I would write—sometimes with a question, eventually to have her review an article I was writing. This time was different, however. I had some good news to share. I had just returned from Omaha, Nebraska. The directors of the Hudson Center for Brief Therapy, Patricia and Bill O'Hanlon, had offered me a job.

The response from Insoo came swiftly in the form of a phone call. "Scott?" I remember her asking, "This is Insoo, Insoo Berg, from BRIEF in Milwaukee". Actually, I recognised her voice instantly from both the accent and enthusiastic tone. She continued, "I received your letter. I hope I'm not too late".

The urgency of the last statement took me by surprise. "Too late?" I responded. "Yes!" she said emphatically, and then came directly to the point: "Before you take that job in Omaha, why not come to Milwaukee and visit us for a few days? We happen to have a job open here". Within a week, I was on my way.

I can still remember the surprise I felt when I arrived. At the time, I was living in sunny, upscale Palm Springs, California and working at a new, privately-owned and beautifully furnished psychiatric hospital. The city of Milwaukee immediately struck me as dumpy and run-down, and my first impression of BFTC was no different. The clinic that was influencing so many around the world did not sit atop the newest, centrally-located building in the city. It occupied the ground floor of an old office building in a gritty, working-class neighbourhood. And the furnishings? Straight out of the 1960s: dark wood panelling, Eisenhower-era desk chairs on casters, and World War II surplus metal desks.

What could I say? I *loved* it. The Center was a hive of activity. Therapists hailing from a number of different countries buzzed about, watching live sessions, discussing cases, and attending lectures and discussion groups. One large room with multiple one-way mirrors made it possible to watch up to three interviews with clients simultaneously. Then there were the clients. They were different from any I had ever encountered. Brother Joel and Father Tom, both of whom lived and worked with the downtrodden in the inner city, brought people in right off the streets for therapy.

One session from that time still sticks in my memory. It was late in the afternoon. Insoo was in the consulting room awaiting her next client. Everyone, me included, was perched behind the one-way mirror anticipating the visit. The door finally opened and in walked Brother Joel. He was struggling to support a man who was either high or intoxicated and, judging by his appearance, very probably homeless. Relief swept across all of us who were watching when the pair finally made it to their seats.

As Insoo began the interview, the man's head continuously bobbed up and down. Eventually, he lost consciousness and began to slide out of the chair. I can remember thinking, "this guy is in no condition for therapy". Standard wisdom then, as now, is that one cannot treat a person "under the influence". Not true for Insoo. She turned to the mirror and, for the first time I had ever witnessed, talked directly to the team. "Hey," she said and then motioned impatiently with her hand, "some of you big guys sitting back there, come in and help us". Several of us, me included, immediately joined her, Brother Joel and the man. Insoo then turned back to the client and began tapping him vigorously on the knee. "Ha ... lo ... ohhh," she shouted in a friendly voice. Tap, tap, tap. "Haaa ... lo ... oh." Tap, tap, tap.

The moment the man stirred back to life Insoo instructed us to grab him under the arms and begin walking around the room. Several times the man's knees buckled and we were forced to bear his entire weight. "Keep movin", Insoo demanded, and then began tapping the man on the shoulder. "I'm Insoo", she continued as if everything were normal, "what's your name?" Personally, I could not understand a word he said when he did speak.

"Ha-le-ah-wu ... hoo ... ick," he mumbled. "Exactly" I thought to myself, hoping it would all come to an end soon. The smell of alcohol and the streets was overwhelming. Alas, it did not. Indeed, Insoo persisted for more than an hour. And along the way, the most remarkable transformation took place. I would not have believed it had I not witnessed the session myself. By the end, the man, Insoo and Brother Joel were engaged in a lively and coherent conversation about his problems and plan for the future. "It's hard work", Insoo said later when discussing the session with the group, "but what else can you do? This may be the only chance I get, so I keep trying."

Hard work and persistence. Two important values both of which were confirmed when I left my cushy job in Southern California to work at BFTC. We worked every day, from 8:00 a.m. until 8:00 p.m., or later, including Saturdays and many Sundays. Luckily, I was single at the time. Not surprisingly, I remained so until I left the Center some five years later!

Another core principle was collaboration. Most tasks were truly a team effort. We taught together. When one of us met a client, the rest watched, coached, and brainstormed behind the one-way mirror. Given the hours we kept, we frequently ate together (this of course provided us with more time to work!). That first week I visited BFTC to interview for the job, I had an experience with Steve that foreshadowed the work that would follow. "Read this", he said in a stern tone, while simultaneously pushing a handful of pages in my direction, "tell me what you think".

Needless to say, I was a bit uncertain about what to do. After all, I was at the Center for a job interview—a job I wanted. Was I supposed to show what I knew? Show how impressed I was with what "the boss" knew? Applaud regardless? Make cogent criticisms? Eventually, I decided to simply state what I thought.

"Harumph," Steve responded, sounding exasperated. "Come with me," he said. I followed, of course, petrified, and then stood motionless by his desk as he sat down. "What did you say?" he asked in a gruff, commanding voice. I could hardly speak and was still spluttering when he sighed loudly, swung round in the chair, and turned on his computer. Thumbing through the pages, he found a section where I had made some notes in the margin. I was shocked when, after reading what I had written, he erased his own text and inserted mine. Then, as he turned around to face me once again, he asked, "What else?"

Even now, nearly 20 years after leaving Milwaukee, I strive to live by the principles that so much informed the work of de Shazer, Berg, and the team at BFTC.

Scott D Miller Ph.D is founder and director of the Center for Clinical Excellence, Chicago, USA. He is an international trainer and supervisor and co-author of *Short-term Treatment of Alcohol Problems* and *The Miracle Method* with Insoo Kim Berg, and a Consultant Member of the "Evolution of Psychotherapy" conference.

Thorana S Nelson   Utah, USA

Memories

Writing about my experiences with Insoo and Steve conjures up all kinds of images. Some are of learning times: watching them work; listening as they described what they thought was going on in the work or in their heads; reading many articles, chapters, and books. Other images are of social interaction. I think those were also learning times because they seemed to involve talk about the work as well as about music and travel and other topics. They seemed to embody a solution-focused life. One of the things that interested me most was how different Insoo and Steve were in their styles. This helped me understand that I could embrace the approach within my own style.

I met Steve when I chaired a workshop for which he was the invited speaker. I studiously read his first book (de Shazer, 1982), which we had been using in our graduate training program, experimenting with practices such as the formula first session task. Many years later, when we met for the Hammond, Indiana seminars, I reminded Steve when we had first met. Sometime later, he said, "Iowa City". Others in the group looked puzzled, yet that was indeed where we had met and had a brief lunch together. His mind had stored what I thought would be very esoteric information.

I am not sure when I first met Insoo. I recall chatting with her in the late 1980s at a conference in Indiana where she was the main speaker. I was fascinated with her manner, so different from Steve's, and what she was showing about the approach. She was quite gracious and, some years later when I asked her if I could spend a few days with her in Milwaukee, she indicated that she remembered me and would be delighted to have me behind the mirror at BFTC. My time there was memorable on many levels, not the least of which was her graciousness as a hostess: we had takeout Chinese for dinner at her house.

Many writers in this book are recalling situations around food with Insoo and Steve, particularly when Steve cooked. When I visited Milwaukee with Steve, we had takeout pizza. I wonder if that's a theme of which I should take note. However, I still have a file of "Steve's brat recipes" on my computer. We always enjoyed dinner at Yvonne Dolan's and Terry Trepper's house during the Hammond meetings and one time, Steve fixed bratwurst and sauerkraut for us in many variations.

Solution-focused thinking has influenced my life in many ways. At first, it seemed to be an interesting way of approaching therapy, one that eschewed protracted conversations about problems, an approach I have always given wide berth to as not much fun. Notions of exceptions and scaling made intuitive sense and I know that "what the client wants" is what is most important in therapy. I assure clients that others have perspectives, but so do they, and Steve's ideas of 'binocular' vision (de Shazer, 1982) and Insoo's unflappable faith in clients echo as we talk about how they can move on in life.

I'm not well versed in Wittgenstein's writings or formal notions of language games, although I did very much appreciate *Words Were Originally Magic* (de Shazer, 1994) and consider myself poststructuralist and think I know the difference between theory and Theory, between explanation and description. Solution-focused ideas have influenced my therapy and therapy training practices immensely. I'm a bit of a cynic by nature, and pushing myself to actually see things differently from the way I saw them 30 years ago has been a gratifying journey. By firmly believing in equifinality (the systems concept that we can arrive at similar points through many paths), that I do not need to fix what's not broken, and that if something is working to keep doing it, I am able to provide encouragement and mentoring to therapists in training regardless of which therapy approaches they prefer for their own work. Of course, I'm delighted when they wish to use SFBT, but I can help them learn what works for them through solution-focused supervision.

Personally, I try not to "do therapy" with friends and family, but one time, when my daughter was quite upset, I asked her simply, "What do you want?" She took several moments during which I could see her thinking hard and "looking" at different possibilities. She finally answered with a clear and confident picture of what she wanted and how it would be different from her current struggle.

Solution-focused thinking has changed how I approach situations in my own life, also. When faced with dilemmas, I have learned to be patient, to scan for exceptions and successes in similar situations, and to clarify a picture in detail of a life without the difficulty and what I am doing in that picture.

My favourite practices in solution-focused work go beyond ideas of what the client wants, exceptions, and small changes that lead to bigger ones. I mostly like involving important others in clients' systems, either in the room or in the conversation. My early training as a systems therapist is well ingrained and I believe that this thinking was important for Steve and Insoo as well. Using solution-focused practices in systemic ways, understanding that the Miracle Question is a process, not a single question is very important to me. Relationship questions such as, "Who would notice?", "What difference would that make to them?", "What difference would that make to you?", and "What else?" are incredibly important for me. But all of those things – exception, scaling, miracle and relationship questions – fit best within a paradigm of solution-building rather than problem-solving thinking.

I have learned well that solution-focused work is simple yet not easy. I have written about the basic assumptions, concepts, and practices many times and still find that sometimes I must be still and trust the approach as clients do their work. Steve and Insoo were anything but simple, as far as I am concerned. They embodied a non-pathologising approach to life and helping people with their problems and led the way for us to think and work differently. On the surface, the product looks simple, yet it took them years and years of reading and talking and practising and talking some more, finding ways of describing what clients were teaching them. They would say that many of the writers in this book as well as many, many others (in addition to clients) are as responsible as they are for how the approach looks today in its different forms. The simple idea of asking about existing solutions that may have gone unnoticed rather than suggesting or directing new ones created by therapists was ground breaking and lives on through the work of people all over the world. I am humbled to be a small, small part of that work.

References

de Shazer, S. (1982). *Patterns of brief family therapy: An ecosystemic approach.* New York: Guilford.
de Shazer, S. (1994). *Words were originally magic.* New York: WW Norton.

Thorana S Nelson is a psychotherapist in private practice in Utah, USA.

Plamen Panayotov   Rousse, Bulgaria

Parting with Insoo and Steve

A group of joyful and friendly therapists from around the world got together before parting. It was the last night of our one-month training at the Brief Family Therapy Centre in Milwaukee. Andrew-Kim, Christina, David, Eun-Sook, Insoo, Ivanna, Ivar, Klement, Molly, Moon-Ja, Morten, Plamen, Steve, Theresa and Thomas talked for a while until almost midnight on 24 August 1994.

Here is part of what Insoo and Steve shared with us that night.

About Each Other

Question: Insoo, what is the most important thing about Steve people should know, and Steve, what is the most important thing about Insoo?

Steve: Well, Insoo is a very good person, and just speaking professionally, if you want to watch a Master Therapist, you should watch her work ... and then try to figure out how the hell she and her clients do it. That's what I've been doing the last twenty years in my work ... She and her clients somehow do this thing ... and I was trained in a rather hard version of sociology, where everything was supposed to be counted and identified properly ... that isn't the way therapy is. But it's clear she is a Master at this. And a very creative listener ...

Insoo (laughing): You should say "hard working".

Steve (laughing): And hard working ... well, "the most important", not "the worst" thing about you. It might be important, but I put "hard working" in a slightly different category from "important" ...

Insoo: I know you do. I think that's a good value, but you don't ...

Steve: Well, I think that it is a good value, but there is a line between "hard working" and ... something else.

Insoo (laughing): Fanatic.

Steve: Okay.

Insoo: Being a fanatic worker – that's me.

Steve: Yes, that's you.

Insoo: I suppose it is my turn to say something about Steve. I think it's been a very good working relationship, because we are so different, very different...

Steve (laughing): Yeah, she is shorter than me...

Insoo: And somehow we had enough maturity, enough sense to figure out how to use these differences, how to combine them. And I think that Steve's clear thinking... I have always admired his ability to think things clearly. I don't know if it's due to his Jesuit education, but he has this incredible ability to do that, and to write things in a very simple manner that is understandable ... We bring differences and fit them together, so it was natural for us to see clients who disagree and fight.

Steve: Yeah, the classical example – couples fight over the toilet paper, should it be rolled over the top or under the bottom, and actually people do argue about that, or the toothpaste, and for me as a result of our being together over the years – that's just the way life is. That is not a problem; it's just the way life is...

Question: So, I wonder, how is the toilet paper managed at your home?

Insoo (laughing): I decide it!

Steve (laughing): It depends who does it ... and we have separate toothpastes!

Insoo: Yes, coming from different cultural backgrounds has been helpful. People see this as problematic, but it's been helpful for us, because we've been able to see the strengths in both cultures, and we try to use these differences, and take advantage of them...

About Holiness

Insoo: We have become fascinated over the years with ... different cultures have different ideas of what is holy, what is sacred. Australian aboriginal people believe there is a spirit in a tree, so they see this tree as very sacred. Native Americans have a similar point of view of Nature. Travelling a lot, we've been studying this. Everywhere we go we love to look at temples, churches, trees, rocks, and oceans ... at what is holy, what is God-like.

Question: So, what is sacred and holy for you two?

Insoo: I didn't realise I was going to be so emotional about this, but I think that in this world there is too much of (weeping) ... disrespect for each other, among human beings, and that is really upsetting. So, I think the reason we spend so much time developing this model has much to do with wanting to show professional people *how to be respectful* of the people they work with ... so, that is what I consider as very holy. What about you?

Steve: That's not a word I use ... I think that throughout history, as far as I can tell reading it, and certainly through our own personal observation, the majority of the time people make the equation "difference = bad", and we have the example today of Yugoslavia. And I think that it is the exact opposite – difference is good, and difference is necessary, otherwise it would be all the same, and that would be boring, at least. So, I value differences, and I am very interested in differences – that is one of the reasons I've been busy and active in this thing called the European Brief Therapy Association. It is a small attempt just among brief therapists, to somehow value the differences. That is why we have these conferences all over Europe, talking to each other about doing brief therapy, whether in Łódź, Poland or Salamanca, Spain, and they will talk to each other, and not fight, and value the differences among them ... I would not attach the word 'sacred' to it, but it has something to do with ...

Insoo: ... with the spiritual side of things.

About Laughter

Question: What do you like doing most in therapy?

Insoo: I would like to see clients laugh. But I don't know if this is always possible.

Steve: That's true. The first thing Joe Burger said the first time he watched therapy was, "you should try to get everybody to laugh at the first session". And I would like to get a laugh if I can, or at least a good smile . . .

About Going On

Question: Do you think it's necessary for us to follow the steps you went through?

Insoo: No, I don't think it's necessary, and I don't think it's useful, either.

Steve: I also think it is not useful . . . People should pick up from where we are, and . . . **go on!** If they are to repeat what we do, then we are in an endless loop, losing time.

About Luck

Question: Is there anything else you would like to tell us?

Steve: You have a nice, interesting plan, hope, dream, and you have to keep that in mind, taking half a step at a time. And when you are taking these half steps at a time, you always need to be constantly aware of things that **accidentally happen** to you. And to take advantage of whatever accidentally happens . . . The miracle question is an example – a client said something about "it would take a miracle", Insoo heard that word "miracle" . . . these sorts of accidents. If we hadn't been prepared to look for accidents like this, we would have never learned to use the miracle question, it would have faded away. . . So, you have to be always aware of accidents, as you are walking your half steps at a time, and take advantage of them. Then the accidents may turn you away from what you think is your final goal, but you end up at another goal that is just as good . . . or better.

Then we wished one another the best of luck, and went our different ways, searching for holy clients to teach us how to help miracles happen, hopefully with laughter or at least a smile.

Plamen Panayotov is a doctor at a psychiatric outpatient clinic in Rousse, Bulgaria. He is Chairman of the Board of Solutions Brief Therapy and Counselling Centre in Bulgaria and a trainer in Solution-Focused Brief Therapy at Kanchev University, Rousse.

Harvey Ratner   London, UK

Insoo: a woman of many parts

With my colleagues Evan George and Chris Iveson, I first met Insoo when she came to London in 1990 with Steve. In advance of a two-day public presentation, they had agreed to spend a day working with us in the National Health Service mental health clinic where we then worked. Evan has written in this volume about encountering Steve for the first time. One of the things that strikes me looking back is the difference between the two: Steve's eccentric appearance against Insoo's very business-like suit, and the differences in their work. Insoo was intense and engaged and highly disciplined, whereas Steve seemed harder to approach, and in the sessions they conducted that day, Steve was less disciplined in his work, launching into an exceptions inquiry after the first thing the client said about the problem he had come with, and then changing tack and going to the miracle question. It was Insoo who appeared more focused and this extended itself to the live supervision of our cases. When I came out for a break from my session, she pointed out that I had not asked the miracle question properly. As someone who had, in those early years, struggled with using the technique, it's perhaps not surprising that this stung me and actually put me off touching it for several months!

However, I recognised that she had been right. I had got it wrong and this was a taste of the directness with which Insoo could state things, and in a way that was more shocking than with Steve; he made no bones about not suffering fools gladly and didn't mind if people decided to take offence, while Insoo would always have her wonderful smile at the ready, and this was so disarming! For example, one time in the 2000s I reminded her of the special edition of Context, the UK family therapy news magazine, which had devoted a special issue to them when they came to us in 1990. On the front cover was an odd photo of Steve and

Insoo standing next to a bust of Freud. When I asked her if she recalled this, because I remembered sending them a copy, she said with a big smile, "oh, that would have gone straight in the rubbish bin!" I was impressed with this indication that she was no hoarder of paper. But that's not a lesson I've personally been able to take to heart!

Over the years it seemed to us that Insoo gradually revealed other aspects that were often surprising. 10 years after appearing in the suit, she presented for us wearing casual clothes and sneakers. But most challenging to our perceptions was when we saw her clinical work. In September 2006 she came in place of Steve, who had for a number of years run live session masterclasses where he saw clients at BRIEF in front of the audience. I believe these are the last recordings of her clinical work, just as we have the dubious privilege of having recorded Steve's last work from the year before. The sessions that she conducted were in marked contrast to the focused and disciplined work she had displayed in 1990 and Steve had been demonstrating to us for several years. Her meetings were markedly longer, and at times she seemed to do little more than listen closely as the clients talked about their problems. I remember feeling impatient, wishing she would reach the miracle question or a scale. She of course knew what kind of sessions Steve had been doing for us, and it was as if she were deliberately demonstrating for us a different, more easy going and, yes, less disciplined style as a perfectly viable model for doing solution focused work. This lesson has stayed with me when I'm teaching and I can sense myself becoming too rigid in the way I'm describing 'correct' SF practice.

The following year, after her death, we arranged an event to commemorate her and Steve's work and we showed extracts from various tapes from our library. Comparing the session of 1990 with that of 2006, Chris made the perceptive comment that in some ways she and Steve had switched positions, in the sense that while he had looked somewhat haphazard in his approach in 1990 compared with her directness, the last work of each showed the opposite characteristics. This, Chris conjectured, was to do with the different paths each took. While Steve preferred to philosophise about the therapy, Insoo was out there on the front line, taking solution focused practice out of the therapy room, and this of course was amply reflected in her many books about different applications. There is a hilarious moment in an interview that Insoo gave where she was asked about her latest interests and she talked about child protection work and the challenges it presented to the solution focused practitioner. She was then asked about Steve and she replied that "he's very interested in the verb 'to be'".

To this day their different positions have continued to influence our everyday practice and teaching. Like so many others we read and reread Steve's philosophically inclined articles and books as we try to fathom how SF works. And it is Insoo's continued search for the practical applicability of the techniques that has guided our work in the many different contexts, from schools to hospitals, where we meet clients.

In the way they balanced each other they were, in a sense, the perfect pair to act as ambassadors for solution focused practice. And there was no doubt about their commitment to each other. I remember Steve at our house after one of his presentations in the 1990s, and he had mentioned that Insoo would be telephoning and he was clearly looking forward to talking to her and looked like an excited youth when she called. After he died, there was a conference in early 2006 on solution focused training that Insoo had organised with Arnoud Huibers in Amsterdam that she had hoped Steve would have lived to be present at. I will always remember how, when we showed the tape of Steve's last session, she watched it while sitting with, I believe, two colleagues from Hong Kong. The next morning as I made my way to the conference hall I passed her sitting on her own in the corridor. I nodded good morning to her but said no more because I thought she looked meditative and I assumed she might want some time alone. But then I noticed that she was in fact crying and I went and sat with her and with her head on my shoulder she talked about Steve.

Harvey Ratner is a brief therapist, supervisor, coach, trainer and founder member of BRIEF, London, UK, and the author of numerous publications.

Gudrun Sickinger   Bremen, Germany

The wonder of the miracle question – you may wonder ...

It was at the beginning of my further training as a systemic family therapist at the North German Institute for Brief Therapy (NIK) that I first met the co-founders of the solution-oriented approach, Steve de Shazer and Insoo Kim Berg. They were to lead one of the key modules of the training as guest speakers and had offered to perform live consultations. We, the participants of the training group, were very excited at the prospect of getting to know the "masters" personally being be able to see them in action. We had already learned some of the basic solution-oriented methods from our trainers and had tried them out in the seminar together.

Shortly before the module with Steve and Insoo, I was commissioned by my previous employer to look after a young woman (about 30 years old), who had to cope with massive panic attacks and was now attempting to start work in the institute's administration department. At that time I was working as a professional counsellor in a large institution for the disabled in northern Germany and I had as yet no experience in the therapeutic treatment of anxiety and panic attacks. So I felt very insecure and had little idea of how I could help this woman. At the initial meeting, in which I uncovered a few details about the symptoms, possible explanations and previous attempts at a solution, and also wanted to clarify my assignment with her, I tried very hard to make use of the solution-oriented approach. This she refused, however, saying that she must first tell me how everything arose, when it started and with what it might be connected. As a budding brief therapist, I did not want to spend much time "digging up" the past, but I asked her politely how much time we should plan for this before we could address her goals. Her answer was decisive and clear, without a shadow of a doubt: "20 sessions". This answer startled me so much that at first nothing occurred to me to say. So I quickly ended the first session to give me time to think about how I could proceed.

While reflecting on this first session, I had the bright idea of making use of Steve de Shazer's offer of a consultation. So I explained to her who Steve de Shazer was, an American therapist who had developed a method that allowed him to help people to transform even serious problems into solutions and thus to overcome them. This made her very curious and she agreed to try it. Because of her fears, she was not able to come alone and so arranged for her mother to accompany her. Her mother, with whom she lived, was in any case already acting as a safety factor in her life; for example, she would wait at the garden gate for her daughter when she came home from work. On the agreed date the two travelled together the 50 km to Bremen.

Everything was ready and waiting at the venue. The two were taken into a conference room, which could be observed through a one-way mirror from the next room. Back then one-way mirrors were still in use, but nowadays they are outdated. In the room behind the mirror sat Wolfgang Eberling, an NIK representative, Insoo Kim Berg and myself. In the seminar room opposite sat the participants of the training group, following the conversation between Steve de Shazer, the client and her mother via a monitor.

Steve de Shazer conducted the interview with the customary questions about exceptions or good and not so good days and the miracle scenario. To the first question, "If a 10 on the scale represents the goal of therapy, and 0 is the situation before the start of therapy", the client rated her current situation at 3. There had also been good days, which she rated at 8 that had occurred about once a month. The miracle was described by the client as follows: the fear regarding the new job would have disappeared, she would travel around town alone at night, and she would have her own apartment and a driver's licence. Regarding the question "What else?" she replied, to live in a partnership of equals and to have children. For the mother, the miracle was evident in that her daughter would travel around town on her own and would do so happily, and she would no longer have to wait at the gate for her daughter to arrive back from work. At the end of the interview Steve asked a question to explore the so-called motivation to change. "If 0 on a scale means you can only hope and pray, and 10 means you will go to any length to bring about a change, where on this scale would you rate your current willingness to work toward a solution?" Both mother and daughter rated their willingness with a 10. The client mentioned that she could do much on her own, but would not feel good while doing it.

Steve de Shazer then took a break and came to us in the next room. I was very excited about how Steve and Insoo would consult and, most importantly, what intervention they would come up with. But first Insoo launched into a rant saying, "How boring, how boring, how boring". I was quite perplexed at her emotional reaction, since I had experienced her so far as a very polite person. Even more surprising, however, was Steve's response: "Shut up!" Short and sweet in a strong voice. There followed a deathly, embarrassed silence. A minute later, Steve turned to Insoo and asked what ideas she had regarding compliments. And as if someone had flipped a switch, Insoo started in a friendly voice, listing a few aspects that had made a positive impression on her. Steve listened to everything calmly, nodding in agreement. Then the two of them developed an intervention for both the client and her mother.

After ten minutes of consultation Steve went back to the client and her mother and presented the intervention. The first task related to the scale used at the beginning of the conversation and was directed at both the client and her mother, namely, that in the evening they should use this rating of 0 to 10 to predict where on the scale the daughter would be the next day. The following evening, both should verify whether their predictions had been correct or not. The second task was addressed to the client's mother: every day at noon to toss a coin, and if it fell tails the mother should not wait at the gate and both should see what difference this made. For the daughter Steve had the following recommendation: on two days of the week to act as if she were at 8 on the scale (this was the highest score she had mentioned), not to tell the mother about this, but to let her guess on what days this was the case.

Since the client and her mother had no further questions, Steve sent them off with a friendly smile. And I was extremely happy that Steve and Insoo had come up with such a clever proposal for the client and her mother.

But the story had an unexpected ending. When I saw the client the following week, she could muster little enthusiasm for her conversation with Steve. In particular, she made fun of the strange questions he had asked, and she wondered what it was all for. Nevertheless, Steve de Shazer's intervention had already had an impact. The mother had taken to waiting for her daughter at the garden gate only irregularly, without tossing a coin, and her daughter coped with this and was able to dispense with this safety factor. At the next meeting, the client reported that she had gone out with a girlfriend and had made the acquaintance of five different men. In the following period, she strengthened the contact with one of these men, who invited her to a holiday to Majorca. Despite her fear of flying she succeeded in surviving the trip and controlling any panic as it arose without outside help. She rated this experience at an 8.

About six months after her consultation with Steve de Shazer, she told me that she was pregnant and had decided to have the child, despite concerns voiced by those close to her. This decision would help her to take responsibility, to do many things more consciously and, on the whole, to be stronger. The occasional appearance of anxiety symptoms with the associated physical side effects she judged quite differently, attributing them as normal feelings associated with her pregnancy. Overall, she rated the improvements at 7 on the scale.

Sometime later, by chance I saw her while shopping with a pram in which her baby daughter was sleeping. She proudly told me about her very good progress since the birth of her daughter. Since then she had finally overcome her anxiety attacks because she did not want to pass on her fears to her daughter. So over the course of a year, the miracle scenario that she had described had become a reality.

Personal Conclusion

This experience has shown me two important things:

Firstly, when I started my consulting career, I thought that experts in communication and counselling, and especially my great role models like Steve and Insoo, were always in a position to control their emotional reactions or even to prevent negative emotions from developing, to handle "difficult" clients without exception in a calm, sovereign manner. This assumption had to be thoroughly revised after the experience with Steve and Insoo as related above. It became clear to me that even "masters" are people with normal feelings. They too can be upset by clients. The difference which makes a difference is probably not to cling to such feelings, but as quickly as possible to switch to a constructive mind set. And that is what both of them managed in just a few minutes (sometimes I need a little longer).

Secondly, I believed at the time that it was important to ask the client questions which were understandable and comprehensible in order to establish a good rapport with them and to promote the development of trust. The experience with Steve and Insoo has taught me that even if clients at first find certain questions to be strange, and perhaps cannot see any benefit in them or consider them absurd, yet they can still have an effect. In this case here, even an amazing effect. This has definitely given me courage during consulting sessions to repeatedly pose unusual questions to clients, even if they do not immediately take to them, perhaps even baulk and express criticism, and yet to trust the effectiveness of such questions.

Gudrun Sickinger is a psychologist in Bremen, Germany. She is an instructional therapist, supervisor and coach at the North German Institute for Brief Therapy, NIK, and an educational therapist / teacher supervisor and instructional coach at the Systemic Society (SG).

Therese Steiner   Embrach, Switzerland

Some memories

At the end of my training in Milwaukee, a participant from Bulgaria interviewed Steve and Insoo, during which personal aspects were discussed. A statement by Insoo stuck in my memory. I quote: "We learned to use our differences not as a barrier but as an enrichment". Very wise and yet so difficult to implement in one's own life!

Yes, there were very considerable differences between the two. Insoo, the small, petite Asian woman, who until her death at the age of 72 was able, while standing, to place both hands on the floor palms down, and in whose face the sun appeared when she laughed. Whoever encountered her felt valued by her and in a very special way welcomed and understood. On the other hand, Steve was a large, gaunt man, with awkward movements and scant eye contact. Based solely on his outward appearance, he could easily be confused with a marginal figure in society. He captivated the interest of his counterparts with his very precise way of speaking and his absolute, focused attention. I have never since met a person whose concentration in an interview was as palpable as was Steve's.

There was a training workshop for therapists who intended to teach the solution-focused approach. This workshop was chaired by Steve and Insoo. Many of the participants had travelled a long way and all had paid considerable money to learn to communicate this approach to others.

At the beginning of the training Steve appeared without Insoo, greeted us warmly, sat down on a chair and said nothing. And he was silent not just for a minute or two; he just sat there in silence for a very long time. The participants became restless, wondering when the training would start. After some time, the first person left the room, disgusted at what had happened. Those who remained were very confused, but started to sense that this silence must have a certain meaning. I cannot remember how long we persevered passively. To me it seemed an eternity. Some participants began to discuss what they would like to learn, so that the training would be useful for them. We started to write down the questions that we wanted to ask Steve and Insoo.

Once we posed the first questions to Steve, he got up and began to share his experiences with us. I cannot remember what questions we asked, nor the answers we received. Vivid, however, is the memory of the discipline and consistency with which Steve started the workshop. I think this was the most enduring lesson which I could learn, namely that in a workshop, the participants' questions are the most important thing. Incidentally, when we began to ask questions Insoo joined in, as amenable and open as ever.

I assume that Steve and Insoo knew exactly each other's respective strengths and gave each other space so that these strengths could bear fruit. In this instance, Insoo held back until we understood what the beginning of a workshop is all about.

When I think of Insoo, lots of little episodes come to mind, short conversations and pictures that have been deeply etched in my memory and still have their effect. In Milwaukee, Insoo interviewed a client who had injured his wife the night before. The big, strong man sat taciturnly in his chair and hardly looked up. He seemed to have no interest in the conversation. It was one of the many moments during my training in the US, where I was extremely happy to be behind, and not in front of, the one-way mirror.

Suddenly, the interview gained momentum. Insoo asked the client how he had managed to stop beating his wife ... he could have seriously injured, possibly even killed her. "How did you manage it?" she asked. "How did you do that?" She looked at him with curiosity and appreciation.

The man sat up in his chair and looked at Insoo for the first time. His incredulous look seemed to ask, "Did someone just say something about what I have done well? Is that humanly possible?" From behind the one-way mirror I too was very surprised to hear that question in this context.

After some hesitation, the man began to tell how he had managed to regain control of himself during yesterday's argument. With each of Insoo's follow-up questions, it became clear that he possessed abilities to emerge from his blind rage, to realise what was happening and then act constructively. Insoo's questions hooked onto the client's self-efficacy and generated hope that, in the future, he could respond in a more controlled manner.

This was one of those moments where I learned that it is possible to fabricate a difference that makes a difference, whatever the situation may be. This way of seeing things has accompanied me during my work in Africa and Central America, and has given me and others the courage, even in seemingly hopeless situations, to seek the smallest steps towards change.

And then there's this picture of how Insoo visualised the attitude of "not-knowing" in workshops. She stood beside a seated participant, whom she asked to adopt the client role, she bent her knees so that her eyes were on the same level as the other person and said, "Look through the client's eyes: you will then experience the way that he sees the world and what is important to him. That's what counts!" In my work with children this requirement has often served me well. It really is worthwhile, now and again, to look at things from the child's perspective.

Therese Steiner is a child and youth psychiatrist in private practice in Embrach, Switzerland. She is an international trainer, and doctor for *Terres des Hommes* in Africa and South America. Co-author with Insoo Kim Berg: *Handbook of solution focussed work with children*, author of *Assuming for the moment . . . Suggestions for solution-focused work with children and youth*.

Philip Streit   Graz, Austria

So dry, so warm, so austere, so emotional – Steve de Shazer's exciting therapy

It was in 1994, towards the end of my family therapy training, that I first came across Steve's name. There was a sociologist in Milwaukee, USA, proposing that the imagined visit of a fairy or a wizard in the middle of the night could solve problems. The next morning one just needed to indicate the progress made on a scale from 0 to 10 and everything would be already solved. No tedious problem analysis, but rather a deconstruction of the problem, by constructing, imagining or inventing the solution – more of what is effective in achieving success, rather than highly complex interventions. Ingeniously simple: that is the solution-oriented approach of Steve de Shazer. We were excited, emotional, fascinated even, and we experimented. But, to begin with, we couldn't get the hang of it. It takes a lot of hard work, dedication and practice to apply solutions adroitly, so that the power of a small change can be felt.

The man from Milwaukee remained for me, an apprentice of systemic therapy as I then was, a phenomenon, but I realised that this therapeutic approach worked – written down and made accessible in down-to-earth books.

In mid-2001, encouraged by the great success of a workshop with the author of *Provocative Therapy*, Frank Farrelly, I mustered up the courage and wrote an e-mail: "Dear Mr de Shazer, I would be very happy if you could conduct a three day workshop on Solution Focused Brief Therapy in May 2002 in Graz. Please let me know your fee. I look forward to your reply". Three hours later came the laconic reply: "O.K. I'll come. 2500 + flight and hotel". I was thrilled and busied myself with the preparations at the Institute for Children, Youth and Family. In no time we had over a hundred registrations; at the end, more than one hundred and seventy participants had booked. In November I wrote another e-mail to inform Steve de Shazer about the progress of the preparations. This time there was no answer, not even by Christmas and New Year. Silence on the net. Four weeks before the event and still we had heard nothing: we were really nervous – was he coming or not? I tried to trace him on his European lecture tour, but the phenomenon Steve de Shazer had always just moved on as I tried to reach him. In desperation, I turned to his wife, Insoo Kim Berg. I have rarely had such a friendly conversation with one of the great therapists of the 20th and 21st century. She tried to reassure me and told me straight away: Steve was like that and if he said he would come, then he would come. But she assured me that she would personally take care of the matter.

No answer came until the day before the workshop was due to begin. I had with difficulty been able to find out that Steve de Shazer was supposed to be arriving by train and would then be at the hotel. The hotel called punctually at 16:30; an American named Steve de Shazer had just checked in. I rushed there and found him in his hotel room, where he said to me in his dry, quiet manner, "You send my wife Insoo half way round the world to find me. If I say I'll come, then I'll come. When does the workshop start tomorrow and where do I need to be?" No more, no less. There I stood, ashamed and horrified at the same time, highly excited and full of emotion. I had not trusted him, but there he was, just as agreed.

Things continued in the same vein at the workshop. In incredibly clear and concise language, redolent with sobriety and analytical acumen, Steve de Shazer presented his theoretical system. In his terse and brilliant manner, he trotted through the workshop. It was interesting to observe that the participants were agitated, emotional, excited. Steve de Shazer also spoke little in the breaks, such as during lunch hour. However, one thing soon became clear: Steve loved dry red wines and, interestingly, he always selected the right wine from a menu that for him was just a "German jumble". His question was not, "Does this wine go with the food?" but rather, "What can we eat to go with this wine?" I was excited and, after the fiasco in the hotel room, tried to arrange everything as well as possible. When Steve asked for a volunteer client, I saw my hour had come, entertaining the secret hope of luring him out of his reserve. I asked my most difficult client whether he would be prepared to participate in a live demonstration with Steve, and he gladly agreed.

The therapy session began with the inevitable question: "If 0 represents the start of your therapy sessions with Philip and 10 means that all the problems that led you to Philip have been solved, where are you today?" At that moment I wanted the ground to swallow me up, saying to myself, "If my client now says -2, I can forget everything and pack my things immediately". However, my client said 7, and could hardly be restrained in his flood of words, detailing everything that had changed and improved — all those things that I had tried in vain to find out in the last therapy sessions. My client left the stage strengthened and beaming. Afterwards, I asked him how he could suddenly rate his progress when before with me he never wanted to talk about targets. My client, a bright engineer, chuckled, "It just slipped out, but it feels good. I really have changed something and the way Steve de Shazer does therapy has inspired and motivated me". And that coming from a client who previously had hardly a good word to say about therapy.

Since then, I have posed this scaling question to hundreds of clients to open the so-called "second hour", as Insoo Kim Berg calls it, and the enthusiastic response has brought success. I owe this to my encounter with Steve de Shazer. This man knew how to arouse my emotions. In my opinion this is the secret of Solution-Focused Brief Therapy. This approach may be down-to-earth but it is nevertheless ingenious, positive and forward-looking. The art of Steve de Shazer's approach to solution-oriented brief therapy resides simply in awakening positive emotions. It is not the austere analysis that is decisive, but rather the magic of the positive emotions which are aroused through de Shazer's style of questioning, the power of emotion inherent in his approach. This is the fertile soil for nurturing specific change by means of precisely targeted questions and interventions.

Philip Streit PhD is a clinical and health psychologist, psychotherapist (SF), director of the Academy and Institute for Children, Youth and Family, Graz, Austria. He is a member of the board of directors of the International Positive Psychology Association (IPPA).

Vratislav Strnad   Prague, Czech Republic

Paradigmatic Tension evoked by the SFBT of Steve and Insoo

I am remembering the year 1991 in Hamburg, the first time I met Steve. I was in a Chinese restaurant with Steve, Kurt Ludewig and other colleagues. We ordered meals which we later shared by spinning the round middle part of the table. Steve proposed that we comment with one sentence at every spin of the wheel. A great language game! And me as a bright beginner in SFBT and simultaneously a prisoner of something like that. I remember Steve saying, "The chickens have already lost their teeth". Then somebody else said, "Then, we can only be silent about them, Steve!" I had not a clue about the context even though everyone was shrieking with laughter! Then, it was my turn. What was I supposed to do? Well, I awkwardly said, "If I may, I would like to have some." They all grinned with amusement and probably thought that my comment was caused by hunger behind the Iron Curtain. Only today do I understand that doing what I did wasn't far from the Wittgenstein and SFBT line. But back then I was full of hunger, embarrassment and also of a certain aversion towards this kind of intellectual game. I had not yet come to understand how deeply natural this approach is.

Between 1992 and 1998 Steve visited Prague five times, sometimes with Insoo. He was always very dedicated and selfless. In 1995, they came for a four-day supervision seminar that took place in three different therapeutic sites in Prague. The 30 hours of videos on rotting VHS tapes show that Steve and Insoo didn't always agree. The most distinct example was the mutual discussion about the number of steps a closing intervention should consist of: "There is a bridging point there!" insisted Insoo. Steve kept his minimalist schedule and stayed backstage. I find traces of Insoo in Prague more in her female endurance to follow the same principles than in the philosophical heritage to the practice.

If the systemic therapy presented by Kurt Ludewig and the ISS Hamburg team in 1990-1992 meant a phantom from another world to us (the dust of objectivist thinking, scattered by the family therapy thoughts of Whitaker, Andolfi, Satir, Hoffman and others, had already been stirred), the arrival of Steve set the dust on fire. Still we never became blind followers of Steve and his SFBT in the Czech Republic, either as individual people or in the institutes. Interestingly this is changing only today! (Unlike in neighbouring Poland, where SFBT put its roots down much earlier.) Moravia in particular is a place where some groups of systemic colleagues value SFBT enough to choose this approach as their main identity. Speaking for our institute ISZ-MC in Prague, we are as "behind" as all our other colleagues in the Czech and Slovak Republics (both countries are closely connected both in the training programmes of our institute and in other linkages). We are rediscovering the SFBT principles in a new dimension, although we never left them during the years and never stopped practising it. The primarily perceived pragmatic straightforwardness of SFBT principles is now filling a depth, that wasn't fully realised before ...

If the emotions are perceived as conditions (starters) of behaviour, their reification takes place. However, if we don't perceive emotion as a condition but as a reason to act, it turns us back to where one heads, towards where one goes, what one wants. This is Wittgenstein's key message. The only remaining thing is whether we dare to take it seriously enough.

(If I may add a word on my own behalf about the etiology of the word "WHY?": In the Czech language WHY (*pro?*) is the transparently shortened form of FOR WHAT. In German it is seemingly a shift between WARUM and WO-R-UM. (This is much more a task for German linguists than for me, of course.) The English WHY has its roots in the Old English word HWY, which comes from HWIE – which has conjoint roots both in the West Germanic HWIU and in the Proto Germanic HWI – which means WITH WHAT (WHAT FOR?). In any case, there is no reason to think that WHY must refer back to the Prime Mover etc . . .)

For Steve and his colleagues, as well as for Wittgenstein, emotions are closely connected to actions. I think that this is immensely important for doing psychotherapy, social work, counselling, coaching or whatever work you do. Again, *it is just a focus to depth, just in a different area*! I consider this to be the key importance for practising SFBT – part not only with the passion of analysing problems but with causality as such. This parting cannot be just situational or partial, it needs to be total – for the whole life of us as therapists as people. It brings vertigo, charm and an overwhelming richness.

Recently I was given the honour of reviewing the Czech translation of the last book written by Steve and Insoo together with Yvonne Dolan, Harry Korman, Terry Trepper, and Eric McCollum: *More than Miracles: The State of the Art of Solution-Focused Brief Therapy* (de Shazer et al., 2007). As you may know, this is the last word from the honourable team that had been crucial for Milwaukee BFTC since its beginning. We all – even here in Prague – have known their importance since 1992. I appreciate the enormous heritage this book gives us! We already have two new methodologies inspired by this book and the cooperation behind it.

I am convinced that the thinking and practice of Steve and Insoo's SFBT in the Czech Republic and Slovakia is only waiting for full recognition and appreciation. If we are at six on the imaginary scale, eight is already pulling from the horizon: feeling – thinking – therapeutic action. The fact that Steve "confessed" to the theoretical background of otherwise purely pragmatic SF approach incorporated him into the European thought tradition that follows from the ancient Greeks – since the Greeks were the first to discover the sense of novelty and curiosity of a question. As it is for all of us in Europe and in America, not to go into cultural comparison with other countries, where Steve and Insoo presented and anchored SFBT. There are at least four institutions primarily based on thinking and practising SFBT in the Czech Republic. Only five years ago there was just one (our institute).

Steve and Insoo, simply – THANK YOU. You are here in our work (and in our hearts).

Reference

De Shazer, S., Dolan, Y. M., Korman, H., Trepper, T. S., McCollum, E. E., & Berg, I. K. (2007). *More than miracles: The state of the art of solution-focused brief therapy. Binghamton NY: Haworth Press.*

Vratislav Strnad is a psychotherapist, supervisor and coach in Prague, Czech Republic. He is Director of ISZ-MC Prague, and a coach of systemic and narrative therapy and coaching.

Peter Sundman   Helsinki, Finland

"Be creative!" – Steve' s motto for how to develop solution-focused practice

Steve took part in the discussion on the SFT-L list (an open internet-based discussion forum for the solution focused community) from time to time. It seemed that he read the list regularly and used it to comment on issues that interested him, as well as to keep in touch with friends of his (usually joking).

The following authentic message from Steve on this list is one of my fondest memories of him. It has guided me ever since in how we describe the way solution focused ideas have developed and how we can continue the process. In fact, he seems to encourage us to go on! Steve's message has also another interesting point; it is a clear message to keep focusing on the practical work, not the model or any theory.

On the 8th of November 2000 Steve responds to a concern raised by a group of other trainers (Bill O'Hanlon, Matthew Selekman, Ben Furman, Andrew Duggan) that "SFBT can be too formulaic, with a set of 'approved' questions that lead into manufactured pathways". Steve wrote:

"This alas is what happens when a 'practice' is seen as a model – an orthodoxy develops that has little or nothing to do with the original. Insoo's first law has always been 'Thou must be flexible'. As we observed our practice over the years, these 'questions' were the questions that seem most likely to get useful responses. Now, if you can get as useful responses with other questions, great. The next step is to figure out what can happen before that question, i.e. the context and the sequence of question and response. Then to find simple situations in which you can use the new question and see if it regularly leads to

useful responses – if so, then you have something. If not, perhaps you do not want to use it very often if at all. This process take a lot of patience, a lot of time, watching/listening to tapes, etc. But if you end up with a 'new' useful question, it's worth it."

This message conveys clearly Steve's opinion about how Solution Focused practice should be developed. In fact, the message summarises, in Steve's elegant way, how BFTC did their developmental work. Gale Miller, who observed the practice at BFTC for many years as a sociologist, said that the team members regularly brought video tapes from the sessions at the Center to the research team (in later years Steve, Insoo and Gale) for discussion on whether the session contained something interesting to think about or try out. The discussion often ended in a no or yes; this could be tried out in either a similar situation or in a different situation. After that a new tape could be brought in for further discussion. Sometimes one of the team members still continued with personal experiments despite negative opinions from the others (Miller, 2011).

In calling the work at BFTC a "practice" rather than a model, Steve obviously wanted to stress the importance of behaviour and the ongoing interaction. In other works (de Shazer, 1994) and in teaching he avoided talking about 'theory' as much as he could. He never said anything definitive about why the 'practice' works, presumably for the same reasons. Maybe also because of the inductive nature of the process at BFTC. He knew what had worked for them in their context, but nothing more.

So, Steve pushed himself to improve his practice by trial and error type of experimenting and careful observation in his daily work. He urges us to continue in the same fashion. He certainly wants us to be flexible like Insoo, not 'orthodox'!

Here are my points derived from Steve's message:

- Look at your/others' practice, what you/they are actually doing– not the fixed model (explanations)
- Start from something that has been working for you or other skilful people

- Try continuously to observe, reflect and learn
- Be very open to contradictions, exceptions and accidents – "What a coincidence!" as we put it at TaitoBa
- Be systematic and concentrate on one thing at a time
- Be very curious of the professional's questions, reactions, behaviour; what came before and what happened next
- Try to find new ways of doing – accept errors
- Use personal working theories rather than ready formulated theories by others (naturalistic setting)
- Be creative – new developments also come from mistakes and intuitive actions and reactions.

References

Miller, G. (2011). Personal statement at the 3rd International Systemic Conference, Prague 8 – 11 June, 2011.

de Shazer, S. (1994). *Words Were Originally Magic.* New York: WW Norton.

Peter Sundman is a solution-focused brief therapist, trainer and supervisor in Helsinki, Finland. He trained at the Mental Research Institute (MRI) 1985–86 and Brief Family Therapy Center (BFCT) in 1988, and is a founding member and coach at TaitoBa Training Institute, Helsinki.

Peter Szabó   Basel, Switzerland

Time with Steve and Insoo

In January 2004, I had the chance to spend ten days with Steve and Insoo at their home. Insoo and I were completing the manuscript for our book *Brief Coaching for Lasting Solutions* (Berg & Szabó, 2005). Steve cooked for us. He had been ill for some time; he managed the house and, above all, spent time in his study listening to music.

Shopping with Steve

About 40 cm of new snow had fallen and Steve and I drove in Insoo's car. Steve's BMW convertible and the beautiful old Mercedes remained in the garage, because otherwise we would have had to shovel the driveway clear. Steve wanted to prepare coq au vin. Our first stop was the bank in the traditional part of Milwaukee. "I prefer a privately-owned bank", said Steve. The old traditional butcher (of German origin) was a family business, as was the health food store where I got my gluten-free foodstuffs. Steve was very pleased to be able to offer me such a wide range of goods. It came as no surprise that the grocery store we visited next did not belong to a chain, but had been in private ownership for generations.

Steve wanted to choose a suitable cooking wine for the chicken. Anyone familiar with American supermarkets knows what kind of dimensions such stores can have. The section for white wines extended over three aisles with over 10 metres of shelf space on both sides. I thought that, given this choice on display, it should be easy to select a cooking wine. I wanted to get back to the house quickly to continue writing with Insoo. About 30 minutes later, with my assistance, Steve had narrowed down his choice in the wine department to three bottles. Prior to this, we had paced the long aisles several times, having taken out and carefully inspected hundreds of bottles. Steve settled on a Riesling, preferably of Alsatian origin. He also had a clear idea respecting the acidity and vintage of the desired cooking wine. With the same fastidiousness with which he chose a shopping partner, he searched carefully for the cooking wine in which to braise the chicken. Finally, we drove another 45 minutes across town. He wanted to provide a special culinary delight: homemade ice cream, from the one remaining ice cream parlour that was still in private hands. A family store, Steve said, "I've been going there for decades, and nowhere else will you will find better ice cream". And, of course, dinner that evening tasted just wonderful.

Working with Insoo

For hours Insoo and I had read each chapter and then discussed and developed it. A particularly vexing test of our collaboration turned out to be a chapter that Insoo had entitled "We cannot make other people change." The book was supposed to be about coaching. So, in this chapter, I encouraged Insoo to write in more concrete terms about coaching. She then withdrew to her study for a while to rework this chapter. When she handed me back the manuscript, I searched for a long time and in vain for more references to coaching or new coaching case studies. At first I thought she had mistakenly given me the old version, with the original examples from school and therapy. Only at the very end of the chapter did I find the difference that was to make the difference. Here Insoo had lovingly affirmed my request by adding, "Obviously, you can see how all of the above also applies to coaching".

Insoo's leave-nothing-to-be-desired sales philosophy was perfectly vindicated (the book sells the workshop, the workshop sells the DVD, the DVD sells the book), and we were invited to American coaching conferences to present the solution-focused approach. I wanted to involve Insoo in the co-design of our conference session and so I bombarded her with my nagging questions about the conference call for papers. Sometime later I received the appreciative, encouraging answer via e-mail from Milwaukee: "I trust your judgment implicitly. Whatever you suggest, I'll do it – except, maybe, dancing naked on the table."

Reference

Berg, I. K. and Szabó, P. (2005). *Brief Coaching for Lasting Solutions.* New York: WW Norton.

Peter Szabó Dr. iur is a solution focused coach in Basel, Switzerland. He is an ICF Master Certified Coach and founder of the educational forum and SolutionSurfers (Lucerne, Switzerland), and the author of numerous publications including a collaboration with Insoo Kim Berg on *Brief Coaching for Lasting Solutions*.

Frank N Thomas   Fort Worth, Texas, USA

Re-Collections with Insoo and Steve

I work for Steve and Insoo nearly every week of the year. As Archivist for the Solution Focused Brief Therapy Association of North America (SFBTA), I am tasked with preserving the Brief Family Therapy Center of Milwaukee, Wisconsin USA. I watch videos (there are over 200 in the Archive), read manuscripts and transcripts, correspond with colleagues and analyse the collection. One of my goals as Archivist is promoting their contributions while protecting them as people. As I work, I often recall moments with Insoo and Steve as though they happened yesterday...

First Contact: Steve

A lanky man with strange mannerisms approached me at a party in New York City. It was 1985, and the American Association for Marriage and Family Therapy (AAMFT) annual conference was in full swing. I knew we'd never met before, but he walked up to me with purpose and pushed a business card at me. Without a "hello" or "my name is" to start the social exchange, it was an awkward moment. I took the card. But before I could open my mouth to begin a conversation, he turned and walked away, heading toward another unsuspecting person, business card extended. I tossed the card away, taken aback by his abrupt approach and puzzling social behaviour. I related this story to my professor, Brad Keeney, later that evening. Brad immediately began to chuckle and said, "Well, that had to be Steve de Shazer. I just wrote the foreword to his first book – you need to read it". I ordered *Patterns of Brief Family Therapy* as soon as I returned to Texas and devoured it in a few days – it was the Mental Research Institute (MRI) model I knew so well with hints of Ericksonian and strategic therapies. I had just begun my love affair with solution-focused practices.

First Contact: Insoo

The 1989 AAMFT conference was in San Francisco, one week after the major earthquake. I was fortunate enough to sign up for a workshop with a woman I had heard a lot about: Insoo Kim Berg. Insoo's charm and expertise captivated everyone's attention from her opening remarks to the final question-and-answer exchange. I patiently waited in a queue that spontaneously developed when she finished presenting, witnessing many warm exchanges between Insoo and participants. When my turn to greet her came, I told my story of meeting Steve in New York City a few years previous. Her laugh – well, more of a chuckle with a huge smile – told me I was not the first to relate such an encounter with Steve. We promised to keep in touch, as I was working on some solution-focused supervision ideas in which she expressed interest.

Re-Collections

One memorable occasion involved a simple exchange. Insoo was coming to the area for a major conference, so I called her and made an offer: I would pick Insoo up at the Dallas-Fort Worth airport and take her to her hotel if she would detour thirty miles and speak with my family therapy class at my university. She agreed without reservation. Insoo walked into my class, pulled up a stool (I had to help her onto the high chair), and introduced herself: "Hi, I'm Insoo – what questions do you have?" Students were picking their jaws up off the floor and staring in awe at this icon of brief family therapy. Finally Insoo broke the silence, saying, "OK, if that's all the questions you have ..." and started for the door! Everyone began to laugh, and the exchange quickly became lively and inviting.

On another occasion in the early 1990s, Steve walked up to a group of us in a Miami bar. Without saying a word, he sat down next to me and started staring out the window. I asked, "Can I order something for you from the bar?" His response: more staring-out-the-window behaviour. I turned back to the group, not knowing what to say or do to include Steve in the conversation. A full minute later, Steve said (to no one in particular), "Stoli (Stolichnaya vodka), just a shot, with ice in another glass". When I realised he was responding to my offer, I fell all over myself correctly ordering his drink, and from that moment on we began swapping stories about friends we had in common. Only the gleam in his eye told me he was enjoying himself immensely.

Occasionally both Insoo and Steve were vulnerable, an important aspect of any friendship, but I had many more moments with Insoo sharing humour, dreams, and memories. In 1998, the European Brief Therapy Association (EBTA) met in Salamanca, Spain. While other participants were being chased by young calves around a bull ring, Steve, Insoo and I chose to roast meat over an open fire in an old stone shelter nearby and talk about our work and lives. Steve later disappeared to take a walk, leaving without a word of explanation (which was not that unusual), but Insoo continued to disclose her dreams about "what's next?" in her life and work. Staring into a dying fire, we recollected pasts and imagined futures.

In 2006, Insoo gave a series of lectures at my university in Texas. The crowd was so large that we had to expand the venue and were finally forced to turn away people requesting last-minute entry. At the first presentation, the video equipment was malfunctioning, but Insoo took it in her stride. While the audio-visual experts worked all around her, she captivated the audience with stories about clients and their wonderful ability to change. The pace over the two days was furious with few moments of respite, but Insoo never faltered, soldiering on with vigour and charm. After the last presentation, Insoo told me she would like to get outdoors, so I took her down to the Trinity River Trails in Fort Worth and we walked side-by-side for several miles. She was quiet, so we were quiet. When one of us spotted a bird, I tried to identify it; otherwise, we walked in silence. When we returned to my car to head to the hotel, Insoo began to speak of Steve, who had died only a few short months beforehand. Her pain was palpable. Her tears were honest, and so were mine. Our friendship deepened.

Recursive Connections

These are but a few of my fondest memories of these two wonderful people. They were astounding pioneers, theorists, authors and clinicians. But what is most memorable to me is their humanity. Both Insoo and Steve were accessible, and personable. They did not live in ivory towers or limit contact to paid appearances – they invited you to their home, cooked for you, and gave freely of their time. As I view videos of Steve and Insoo, I realise what a privilege it was to know them. Few people will ever see the videos I archive, but thousands were able to enjoy both the expertise and companionship of this remarkable couple. As I archive, I labour in love: collecting the information, re-collecting the memories, and continuously connecting the two.

Frank N Thomas Ph.D is a couple and family therapist, and Professor of Counselling at Texas Christian University, Fort Worth, Texas, USA. He is Archivist of the Solution Focused Brief Therapy Association of North America (SFBTA), where he works to preserve and document the work of the Brief Family Therapy Center in Milwaukee, Wisconsin.

Terry S Trepper   Chicago, USA

"We have chairs here"

The first time I formally met Steve de Shazer and Insoo Kim Berg was in the context of dating their longtime friend and my future wife, Yvonne Dolan. I accompanied her on a weekend visit to their home in Milwaukee, as she and Insoo were to do a training together at the university. I confess I was a bit nervous about meeting them both.

My fears were confirmed when, just moments after our arrival, Insoo informed me that she would be giving me a "grade" at the end of the weekend regarding my suitability to date her long-time friend. The fact that she had said it playfully did not lessen my anxiety. And even though we all had a very pleasant evening together, I was still nervous.

The next morning, Yvonne and Insoo were going to leave early to get to the training site. Being still somewhat intimidated, and worried at the thought of being alone with the great Steve de Shazer, I carefully planned a day for myself in Milwaukee so that I would not intrude on his privacy. After Yvonne and Insoo left, I started to get my things ready to leave as well. Steve looked at me and said, in a rather brusque way, "You can stay if you want. We've got chairs here". I thought that odd, and was confused as to whether this was an actual or obligatory invitation. I didn't take the chance, and instead thanked him, but told him I wanted to do some work-related errands that day, and would be back by the time Yvonne and Insoo returned.

I had no work errands. I spent the day trying to keep busy, so that I wouldn't have to go back, and accidentally disturb him.

I timed my return to correspond to when Yvonne and Insoo would come back to their house. When Yvonne and I were alone, getting ready for dinner with Steve and Insoo, I told her what I had done, how I had spent the day roaming Milwaukee. She was extremely amused. She explained to me that Steve's reminder that there were chairs at his house was his way of letting me know that I was welcome, that he wanted me there.

Later, at the end of that weekend, just as we were leaving, Insoo finally gave me my grade to date her friend: an "A"! As we were leaving, Steve said that anytime I was in town to remember that they had chairs there. Yvonne explained to me on the drive home that I had just officially been let into the Solution-Focused family.

Yvonne and I married, and for the next five years, I developed a very satisfying relationship with Insoo, but even more so Steve. They lived only a few hours from us, and Steve very often would come down and stay with Yvonne and me for a few days while Insoo was travelling. He visited so often, we even teasingly renamed our guest room "Steve's Room." During his visits, we would listen to music, he would teach me the finer points of the Billy Strayhorn arrangements of Duke Ellington pieces, or just share the enjoyment of one of the Bach suites for unaccompanied cellos. He came to enjoy streaming music services, which allowed me to play immediately a track by Miles Davis that he particularly liked.

During the last year of his life, as he became increasingly ill, he came to visit less often, and for shorter stays. One night, in late August, he looked particularly bad. He said he did not feel well, and was going to go home a day early. Yvonne and I tried to get him to stay until the next morning. He said no, he should go. Thinking that he may have been concerned that he was imposing on us, I said, "Steve, you know ... we have chairs here". He only then agreed to spend the night.

Steve left the next morning. A few weeks later, he died in Vienna.

I often think about that first time I met him, with that very understated "Steve de Shazer invitation" into his world. I have come to fully understand that there are many different ways to be connecting, to show interest, to say "let's get to know each other". You can be ebullient, engaging, cheerfully welcoming ... or, as Steve showed me, you can simply remind someone that "We have chairs here".

Terry S Trepper Ph.D is professor of psychology at Purdue University Calumet, Chicago, USA. He is editor of the *Journal of Family Psychology*, co-author with Steve de Shazer, Yvonne Dolan and others, co-author of *More Than Miracles*, co-editor with Cynthia Franklin and others of *Solution-Focused Brief Therapy: A Handbook of Evidence-Based Practice*, and author of numerous books and scientific articles.

Coert Visser   Utrecht, Netherlands

"You don't know what a mountain is, do you?"

Around 2000, I was captivated by the work of Insoo Kim Berg, Steve de Shazer and their colleagues of the Brief Family Therapy Center. The book *Interviewing for Solutions*, which Insoo and Peter De Jong wrote, described a very attractive way of working: solution-focused working. What attracted me in this approach was that in it I recognised certain elements which resembled how I, on occasions, had already been working as a consultant. I thought the dialogues in the book were fascinating, especially the dialogues which featured Insoo.

While reading, I thought it would be very pleasant to talk to someone who was so friendly and appreciative. The name Insoo somehow seemed to sound Scandinavian to me and I half-consciously visualised a rather tall blond woman. When I finally met Insoo in 2003, I smiled. Insoo turned out to be a Korean name and Insoo was neither tall nor blond. But otherwise my predictions about Insoo had been right. My colleague Gwenda Schlundt Bodien and I launched our own first solution-focused training for coaches and consultants in 2002. In a moment of boldness, we had written Insoo an e-mail asking if she'd like to be one of the trainers in our training. To my surprise and joy she immediately agreed. Insoo joined and blew our participants and us away with her skills and personality.

Another time, in 2004, I had invited her to come and do a master class about solution-focused work for non-therapists in Driebergen in the Netherlands, where I live. Most of the more than 50 attendees were managers and coaches. I had invited her by e-mail and, as before, she just agreed without asking any questions. I thought it would be rather impolite and perhaps not very solution-focused to ask her what she would do in that workshop. Somehow that might be disrespectful. On the day of the workshop I went to pick her up at the airport in Amsterdam. On the drive to Driebergen, which lasted about 40 minutes, I was kind of nervous, wondering whether Insoo had understood my invitation well. Did she understand that the whole workshop revolved around her? Had I made it clear that the participants came only for her and that she would be in front of the group the entire day? What a fool I was! Had I made it clear that these participants weren't therapists? Had I explained that quite a few participants did not know much about the solution-focused approach?

We drove into Driebergen and while she was saying what a lovely village this was, I decided to timidly check, "Insoo, do you have an idea about what you'd like to do with the group, today?" She smiled and said, "Oh, yes, I do". I left it at that, still nervous. Fifteen minutes before the master class was to start, Insoo was going through some pieces of paper she had brought along. I thought to myself, Oh my God, only *now* is she thinking and deciding what to use!" She did it quickly and started the programme. The minute she started my nervousness was gone. She was very confident and the group was all attention. The day was marvellous. It was very interactive. She responded to questions from the group and developed impromptu exercises with them.

Afterwards, Insoo joined me at our house and while I sat down with a few guests on one side of the room Insoo went to another side and, to our surprise, she lay down on the floor and started to do yoga exercises. After dinner we talked and Insoo told me some stories and anecdotes. She talked about Steve and how he loved Shostakovich. He and Brian Cade (if I remember correctly) would sit and listen to Shostakovich loudly and Insoo would go upstairs. She said she preferred softer music, like Mozart. Later, when I drove Insoo back I asked her, "Do you see the solution-focused approach as a *finished* approach or do you think it will keep on developing and changing?" She started laughing and answered right away in a don't-be-silly kind of way, "Oh no, it's not finished. For any model to stay alive it will need to constantly keep developing and renewing itself". She smiled brightly and continued, "So, we need bright young people who will do that". I thought that was an impressive answer. Sometimes when people have developed great things they can become kind of defensive when other people suggest improvements to it. Not Insoo. I thought about her answer. "Bright young people who will do that." Was that an invitation to me? I did not dare ask.

Insoo was every bit as appreciative and friendly as I had imagined. I consider it a privilege to have known her and to have worked with her. That she was authentic in her message appeared from what she did and what she said, even when she was *not* standing in front of a group. She was dead serious about the solution-focused approach. But that does not mean she was all seriousness. On the contrary. She laughed a lot and had a contagious sense of humour and a nice way of teasing people. In 2005, we co-organised a conference on solution-focused training. In an e-mail exchange about that conference she once wrote, "What are the principles of marketing? I guess I am just too relaxed today after a long walk we took in the mountains. (Ooops! You don't know what a mountain is, do you?)".

Although she was friendly and gentle, she knew exactly what she wanted and she knew how to get something done by people. She once told me she had said to someone she'd worked with, "You're going on vacation *again*? You're *so* lazy!" It would surely be impossible to be mad when she would say something like that because she would say it with the nicest smile. But perhaps telling this story was intended to warn me that I should not be lazy when working with her? Well, that warning would not be necessary anyway because it was an energising experience to work with her. I co-wrote several small articles with her. With one of them, I had written a nice – I thought – introduction about people management. Insoo read it, and said, "Oh, this part is a bit overwhelming, to me". We changed that section by making it simpler and thereby making it better. Afterwards, I wondered whether instead of 'overwhelming' she had just meant 'no good'. But I concluded that even if she had meant 'no good' I still would prefer 'overwhelming'. After that, whenever Insoo said 'overwhelming' about something I paid careful attention about what we should change. Usually this this would make things better.

On 11 January 2007, I put my youngest son to bed and I enjoyed reading a story to him after a busy workday. While I was reading I heard my mobile ringing downstairs. Cheerfully I thought to myself, "That person can leave a message", and I read on. But the damn thing kept ringing. Walking downstairs I thought to myself, "Who can be calling at this time? It must be something urgent". When I picked up my phone I saw it was Gwenda, my colleague. I answered the phone and all I heard were three words: "Insoo is dead ..." I fell silent.

Reference

De Jong, P., & Berg, I. K. (2001). *Interviewing for Solutions.* Belmont, CA: Wadsworth.

Coert Visser is a psychologist, coach and trainer in Driebergen, the Netherlands. He is the founder of Solution Focused Change of the Netherlands, a consultant and coach, and author of numerous publications.

Manfred Vogt   Bremen, Germany

A question of attitude

> "The only wisdom
> we can hope to acquire
> is the wisdom of humility:
> humility is endless."
>
> *T. S. Eliot, Four Quartets*

To meet Steve and Insoo meant to meet yourself.

"Thank you for coming!
I hope our session turns out to be in some way useful for you.
There are no guarantees.
But I will do my best!"

Steve started most of his consultations with these words. In my opinion these sentences express the main issues of solution focused brief therapy:

- Gratitude
- Appreciation
- Goal orientation
- Modesty and humility.

The meetings with Steve and Insoo were very valuable for me because they offered a personal and inspiring experience with these abstract terms.

In 1985 Steve and Insoo came to Germany for the first time and I got to know them in a workshop in Hamburg. At that time I was mainly influenced by the systemic approach of the group around Mara Selvini-Palazzoli and the brief therapy approach of the Palo Alto (Mental Research Institute) group around Paul Watzlawick.

Insoo took the opportunity during the workshop to visit Hamburg and to look for a "German car", and so Steve presented many taped sequences of his practical work with clients. It took some time for me to understand how he did his therapeutic consultations. Later on Insoo joined the workshop and presented her own style of working with clients – to some extent similar but also unique.

Steve and Insoo presented with their solution focused approach an intense portion of American pragmatism. I was fascinated by their simple way of dealing with human suffering and other topics of life and these experiences improved my understanding of psychotherapy.

Suddenly the complexity of psychotherapy could be seen simply and well, and translated into a practical conceptualisation of behaviour.

At that time I frequently asked myself what it was that made these two people so extraordinary and interesting for me. Of course it was their methodological processes, their future-oriented questioning, their abandonment of trying to understand problems, their focusing and working out of human strengths and abilities as a basis of building solutions, and their creative and simple interventions. During the workshop I recognised that a respectful and cautious way of dealing with clients was their speciality.

At the time of their first visit to Germany we invited them to our Norddeutsches Institut für Kurzzeittherapie (NIK), which was founded in 1985. We took also the opportunity to visit BFTC in Milwaukee at Steve's invitation. After this visit we started to work more and more in the solution focused way at NIK, and we invited both Steve and Insoo regularly to Bremen and Berlin.

In 1993 Steve suggested that I come to New Orleans, where there was to be a conference honouring John Weakland for his contributions and impetus for the brief therapy approach. In the hotel bar Steve introduced me to Luc Isebaert from Belgium, Marie Christine Cabié from Paris and Anders Claesson from Stockholm. He suggested that we establish a European network of solution focused practitioners. There and then, we made the first step to found the European Brief Therapy Association (EBTA). Over the years EBTA became the main forum for the further development of the solution focused approach beyond the United States.

In the beginning we met regularly every six months at European institutes which had close collaboration with Steve and Insoo too. Then Steve and Insoo encouraged us to organise the first European conference on solution focused brief therapy in Bremen in 1995, to address and include a broader group of interested practitioners. These meetings with many interested and engaged colleagues were an important cornerstone of the development of EBTA. Later on these conferences took place all over Europe annually. Out of these regular meetings a network of friends and colleagues arose.

Through his cautious, calm way of working, Steve taught me how to slow down my own style of interviewing. He emphasised how important it is to observe carefully the behaviour and to listen precisely to the words of the clients. Once he said, "Some therapists behave sometimes as if they seem to have forgotten that listening is a normal thing in every conversation". With this remark he pointed out that brief therapy is always a process of slowing down. At NIK we formulate in this connection "Bist du nicht willig, so brauche ich Geldud" (literally "If you are not willing, then I will use patience"), as a new version of Goethe's famous phrase, "Bist du nicht willig, so brauche ich Gewalt!" ("If you are not willing, then I will use force!").

At one of their European and international intensive summer trainings, which took place at NIK over several years, I invited Steve to the Windjammer parade in Bremerhaven. We discussed the early differentiation of the word games of problem talk versus change talk versus solution talk. After a training with members of a crisis intervention pastoral office in Schleswig-Holstein I was increasingly irritated by this differentiation. During the supervision process with the members of the crisis intervention service it came up that clients, who phoned this service and could express their own problems in words, were often relaxed and relieved through the fact that they were able to express their problems. For these clients the problem talk was a part of their solution. In this training we removed the term "problem talk" and agreed basically to use the word "topic" instead of the word "problem". Topics of life are available in an enormous number. But they must not be a problem. Steve encouraged me to develop a language which did not take the word "problem" as a central part of psychotherapeutic practice.

Later on during a joint holiday on the island of Spiekeroog, Insoo told me about her first experiences as a young Korean woman coming to the United States. She remembered her first feelings as a guest and then as an American and how she looked for her own way between the different cultures. Migration was a relevant part of her life. Steve also had German roots through his grandfather. We often went in the footsteps of his grandfather in Berlin. I was intensely touched by these aspects of their life over the years. My family was forced to seek shelter in new regions several times in the 20th century, due to the two world wars. Out of this I experienced the meaning of feeling like a guest in West Germany in the 1960s.

As migrants we learned in our family how not to attract attention as "refugees". Modesty, gratitude and humility were important virtues. Humility as a possibility of self development and goal orientation had been a leading principle of behaviour for families of refugees in the early sixties, especially after the building of the Berlin Wall. Today we respect these virtues, which we suffered in former times, as valuable resources. In the meetings with Steve and Insoo I understood more and more of my own development. I could reframe my own memories of my childhood and found new explanations.

- Gratitude
- Appreciation
- Goal orientation
- Modesty and humility.

Two weeks before her sudden passing Insoo was once again in Bremen. She told me with a laughing and a crying eye that shortly after her first arrival in the United States, she bought a big grave plot together with her family members to be sure – whatever else happened – that there was a place where she would finally arrive. She joked that his was a good business because in the meantime the prices for graves had gone up dramatically. Future orientation and humour was always a part of Insoo's life style.

It was these conversations and experiences – aside from all the trainings, all the fun and all of the good food – which made the meetings with Steve and Insoo so valuable. It was an encounter with oneself, which reminds me of Nietzsche: "Become who you are!" This message was given by Steve and Insoo over and over again. During the writing of this piece my gratitude to both of them was animated once more. Good memories, thank you!

Manfred Vogt Ph.D is a psychotherapist, child and adolescent psychotherapist in private practice in Bremen, Germany. He is also a family therapist, hypnotherapist, teaching therapist / teacher supervisor and coach at the Systemic Society (SG), a founding member and board member of the European Brief Therapy Association (EBTA), President of the International Alliance of Solution-focused Institutes (IASTI) and the author of numerous publications and therapeutic games.

Michele Weiner-Davis   Boulder, USA

Thoughts of Steve and Insoo

In 1977, I received my Master of Social Work. I marvelled at the fact that someone could receive a master's degree in social work and have learned practically nothing about how to help people change. My head was filled with theories, but void of any practical, effective information about the process of change. Several years into my career, I decided that unless I learned more about how to help people improve their lives, I would quit being a therapist and start a new career.

Fortunately for me, I started reading about Milton Erickson. I was totally enamoured with this new way of thinking. I soon learned that there was a group of people in Milwaukee, Wisconsin, who had developed a model that was based on Erickson's work. This was something I had to check out. And so I did.

I visited the Brief Family Therapy Center late in the summer of 1982. I was greeted by Insoo and Steve. Although a visitor, I was invited to sit behind the one-way mirror and watch them work. Although I was fairly clueless as to what they were doing, I sensed I was on to something big. I decided on the spot to take a nine-month training and Steve was to become my "supervisor".

For the next nine months I drove from my home – an hour and a half drive from Milwaukee – once a week to attend the training. Steve, Insoo and various other team members such as Eve Lipchik, Elam Nunnely, Alex Molnar and Marilyn Bonjean led the pack. As I reflect on my time there, I can honestly say that little has been more exciting than learning the counter-intuitive theories and strategies from Steve and Insoo and the team. I was hooked. It wasn't long before I was a total convert.

I remember a mid-training review with Steve and Insoo when I said, "You haven't given me much feedback about my work", and true to Steve's minimalist style, he replied, "If there had been something wrong, you would have heard from us". So much for concrete feedback. I was hoping for, "You could have done this better, you could have done that better", but in retrospect, they were building on what works.

I distinctly remember another evening when we were reviewing the article written by the staff at MRI entitled *Problem Focused Therapy* (Weakland, Fisch, Watzlawick, & Bodin, 1974). I suggested that we write a corollary article entitled *Solution Focused Therapy*. Steve thought I should write it. I declined. I suggested Steve write it and he did (de Shazer et al., 1986). That article put BFTC as a group on the brief therapy map.

Once the training program was over, Steve invited me to become part of the staff. For the next three years, I did research with Steve and Wally Gingerich. We worked as a team – Steve, the theoretician, Wally, the researcher and me, the clinician. One of us would work with clients and the other two would watch from behind the one-way mirror. The sessions were transcribed and we coded what we and the clients were saying in the hope that we would discover patterns in things therapists do that trigger reports of change, clients' strengths and resources, and hope about the future. And indeed, patterns emerged. It became clear as to what we needed to do to increase the odds that clients would discuss their strengths and solutions. What a thrilling time that was!

As I think back to those times, what really stands out for me, besides the excitement of working with Steve and Insoo and being introduced to many key people in the field, was what I was learning about Steve that few people knew – that he was incredibly kind and nurturing. His awkwardness, aloofness and standoffishness threw people. They thought he was cold and detached. He was anything but. Yet, that is the persona he had with therapists. I remember a panel Steve was on with Bill O'Hanlon at a major conference. Bill called his model Solution-Oriented Therapy. Someone from the audience asked, "Bill, what's the difference between Solution-Focused and Solution-Oriented Therapy?" to which Bill responded, "I make eye contact".

Okay, granted, Steve didn't make eye contact. But a little known fact is that nothing compared to the excitement he felt when clients returned reporting change. He loved it. And from my perspective, he was an incredibly nurturing man. He took me under his wing and mentored me. One evening when I was at the end of my training, he told me that it was time for me to start writing. He said I should go home and write an article over the weekend. I said I would. I wrote an article entitled "Strategies of Parenting", which Steve read the following week and suggested that I submit it to the then Family Therapy Networker. Rich Simon, the executive editor, accepted it almost as it was. What an exciting moment – all thanks to Steve. That was the beginning of my publishing career.

Then, Steve asked me to present with him at the American Association of Marriage and Family Therapy, which I did several times. This gave me enough confidence to begin offering my own workshops. In the same way that Steve was tickled to see changes in his clients, he was equally pleased to witness my contributions to the field. Steve, contrary to popular belief, was a man who was generous of spirit, warm and inspiring.

It's easy to for me to see why many people don't know this about him. His public persona was different. I remember the time that I invited him to do a workshop in my community, long before SFBT was an accepted approach. He showed a tape of himself working with a woman. At the end of the tape, a participant in the audience said, "I just don't get it. How is it that you are not enticed to follow the client's descriptions of the problems and her feeling about the problems?" Steve's response? "I would hate to live in your shoes."

His response belied his depth of wisdom and his incredible ability to teach therapists to stretch beyond their usual ways of thinking and doing things. I cringed because I knew this woman and the others in the workshop wouldn't know the *real* Steve de Shazer.

Years after I left BFTC, I was offered a contract to write a book based on SFBT that helped couples keep their marriages together, called Divorce Busting. I was the first team member to take the concepts and apply them to a particular niche for the general public. Not surprisingly, my book, *Divorce Busting* (Wiener-Davis, 1993), became a best-seller. The world was ready to learn about innovative methods for solving problems, particularly because it challenged the "follow your bliss" thinking characteristic of that era. I helped to put solution focused thinking on the "general public" map. And for that, I received Steve's blessing.

I will be forever grateful for the "brainwashing" I received in the early 1980s and for the opportunities Steve gave me to focus on my strengths within and create my own miracle picture. Thank you, Steve.

References

de Shazer, S., Berg, I. K., Lipchik, E., Nunnally, E., Molnar, A., Gingerich, W., & Weiner-Davis, M. (1986). Brief therapy: focused solution development. *Family Process*, 25(2), 207–21.

Weakland, J. H., Fisch, R., Watzlawick, P., & Bodin, A. M. (1974). Brief Therapy: Focused Problem Resolution. *Family Process*, 13(2), 141–168.

Weiner-Davis, M. (1993). *Divorce Busting: A Revolutionary and Rapid Program for Staying Together. Englewood Cliffs, NJ:* Prentice Hall & IBD.

Michele Weiner-Davis is a former employee at the Brief Therapy Family Center, BFTC, and director of the "Divorce Busting Center", Boulder, Colorado and Illinois.

John Wheeler   Newcastle, UK

Memories of Insoo and Steve

B rief Therapy North East invited Insoo to deliver a two-day workshop in a lecture theatre in Newcastle-upon-Tyne in the UK in 1999. In the UK, workshop presenters often have to prove their credibility before participants, especially front-line practitioners, are willing to learn from them. I looked at the 100 participants looking at Insoo at the front, waiting for her to start, imagining them thinking, "What does this person think she can teach us?" Insoo asked participants to construct a mother and daughter who had come to therapy. Participants relished the opportunity to create the most problem-saturated mother and daughter they could imagine – mental-health issues, substance misuse, sexual abuse and so on. Insoo then invited one half to speak as the mother and one as the daughter. Participants tried as hard as they could to produce replies to Insoo's questions that would make it impossible for her to stay in a position of respectful, hopeful curiosity. Within 10 minutes Insoo had successfully demonstrated the simplicity and potency of the Solution-focused approach, and participants were keen to learn more.

Since then I have usefully recalled this experience when meeting with warring factions – mothers and fathers, parents and teenagers, brothers and sisters. Insoo's example in the lecture theatre gave me the confidence to ask simple questions like, "How would you prefer things to be?" "Suppose x was different in the way you've described, how would that enable you to be different?" "Suppose you were different in that way, how do you think x would react to this change?"

In 2006 a group of us took Insoo out for a meal the night before three days training in Gateshead in the UK. One of us mentioned that she'd been sleeping badly for some time. I asked how long this had been going on for. Insoo asked what she had already tried to deal with the problem.

This small example often reminds me that the opportunities to enquire in a solution-focused way are probably endless. It led me to wonder if solution-focused thinking was in Insoo's bones. And it led me to realise that if solution-focused thinking could be in your bones, it wasn't yet in mine to a reliable extent. Even though I've known the solution-focused approach for 20 years, it appears that I still have a default position of problem focused thinking and taking a solution-focused position is a choice. This encourages me to be mindful of the choices that exist, in many different situations, and to always remember that there is a solution-focused option.

My first experience of Steve was at the EBTA conference in Carlisle in 1999. The plenary discussion became too abstract for some conference participants and Steve, with Insoo, was invited to go on stage to contribute to a discussion on practice. Insoo had commented on the importance of seeing the world through the client's eyes. Steve disagreed. "We can't do that." Steve reflected, "All we have are the client's words". I recall thinking at the time that, "Yes, we can't know life as another person knows it". With some relief I held onto Steve's comment. "However", I thought, "at least we have the client's words, so that gives us something to work with, some way of making a connection, some way of glimpsing how life is for the other person". But Steve hadn't finished. After a thoughtful grunt Steve continued, "And even then we can't know for sure what the client's words mean". A part of me thought, "Damn, that leaves us with nothing".

Steve's brutal honesty about practice has helped me increasingly to let go of illusory sources of certainty when I do my work – what I've learnt about conditions and challenges that beset people, what I've learnt about what people are supposed to do to solve particular problems, my capacity to know how life is for another person. Instead, Steve's comments have helped me to respect the absolute uniqueness of other people's lives, how difficulties affect them, and what it might take for a better life, for them, to come about. The only knowledge that matters at the end of the day is theirs, so my work is to be as helpful as I can in helping them access the knowledge they can have about the changes they need to make and how to make the change happen.

My last experience of Steve was at the EBTA conference in Amsterdam in 2004. Steve was standing on his own as people were taking their seats at the beginning of the conference; lots of people, from lots of countries. I was struck by the energy and excitement in the room, as people met old friends, or talked with people they were meeting for the first time. All had in common an interest in the solution-focused approach and in many cases much more than an interest, a passion. And here was the person who had played such a key part that if he hadn't done all he had done, there would be nothing for these people to be so excited about, in fact, no reason to have a conference at all. A different person from Steve might have expected to be talked to but Steve seemed quite content to just stand in an inconspicuous manner, almost invisible. I went up to Steve and reflected on the energy and excitement in the room, and commented, "I guess it must be pretty rewarding, to know that you've brought something into being that doesn't depend on you for it to keep going".

My comment came from noticing that this doesn't always happen. Sometimes therapeutic approaches are so particular to the person who developed them that no-one else can do it the same way as the origina-tor. For me there's a big difference between someone creating something that works only for them, and someone creating something that can be used by others. When an approach is unique to the origina-tor the best that can be said is "weren't they good". When an approach can be passed on to others, then the possibilities for making a useful difference in the lives of people with difficulties are immense.

Steve responded to my reflection by agreeing that, yes, the solution-focused approach could, and seemed likely to, continue without him having to be involved. This in itself spoke of the immense respect he showed for what others were doing with the approach. A different person might have held on to a position of knowing best how to do solution-focused work, but Steve didn't. For me this spoke of a likeli-hood that not only did he respect that people with difficulties were unique, but practitioners are too, and somehow it's up to us to work out how to get the best out of the solution-focused approach for the sake of the people we work with. Steve then gave a wry smile and commented,

"Maybe it's time for me to move onto another field". Thinking that Steve was referring to his early move from musician to therapist I commented, "What, first a musician, then a therapist, now something else?" "Yes", Steve replied, "I just haven't decided what."

I was left imagining that the person who had been standing in an invisible manner at the beginning of the conference just might move onto another field and disappear from the world of therapy. In a subtle way this also influences my practice. Since coming across the approach that Steve worked so hard to figure out and describe, I've come to realise that if I am to be really helpful to the people I work with, there is only one ego that matters, the client's. The questions I ask may sometimes stand out as being very noticeable because they are so unusual, but what I know about life needs to be very much in the background. The goal for successful work is always that I ultimately disappear and leave people to get on with their lives somewhat more knowledgeable about how to do so – just as Steve seemed ready to leave the world of solution-focused work confident that the people he passed the approach onto will do so in sensible and useful ways.

John Wheeler is a systemic therapist, supervisor and trainer in Ryton, UK. He is co-director of Solution Focused Trainers, and a full member of SFCT – the Association for the Quality Development of Solution Focused Consulting and Training.

Ferdinand Wolf   Hornstein, Austria

Three episodes with Steve de Shazer – personal and professional

In his courses, Steve de Shazer not only taught the solution-focused approach; he epitomised it, as it were, in his very flesh and blood. Through his actions, he could repeatedly surprise his students in a manner that was by turns touching and, occasionally, offensive. Yet he did so in such a way (namely, on the emotional rather than the intellectual level) that they were stimulated to grapple with his methods.

I would like to outline below three episodes that stand out for me as perfect illustrations of Steve de Shazer's consistent stance in all that he did.

"Prwldbdl"

The first episode arose during a live supervision at the Brief Family Therapy Center, Milwaukee, in August 1990, as Steve was working with a female client. He asked in his typical manner, what would have to happen during the session so that the client would perceive a benefit in it for herself and how, in particular, she would notice it. The client answered the question thus: "If our conversation turned out to be useful, I would prwldbdl. "de Shazer continued, "And if you would prwldbdl for some time, what difference would that make for you?" The conversation continued in this way for about 30 minutes until de Shazer took the usual break. He had worked out various alternative scenarios with the client and in order to formulate a concluding message he wanted to hear the opinion of the team of observers, of which I was a member, situated behind the mirror. The first thing he said when he joined us was, "Can anyone tell me, what the hell does 'prwldbdl' mean?" He had made use of the client's expression to structure the interview without knowing what it meant. In fact, he did not have a clue as to which word was being used, since the client had articulated this word so unclearly.

After the break, Steve's message visibly moved the client, who appeared satisfied with the result, even though it had not been ascertained which exact word had been central to the interview, the word upon which, as it were, everything had hinged. This made me realise, once and for all, what "Not-Knowing" means in practice.

"Let them ask questions and let us see what they want!"

In the last four years of his life, Steve de Shazer held an annual seminar for a university course in Solution Focused Coaching and Management in Vienna. I was asked to accompany him, and served in the seminar as his interpreter.

At the first seminar in this series, I asked him if I should make a short introductory statement regarding the solution-focused approach, because I knew that a number of the participants had not attended the course and therefore might have no idea about the concept behind the solution-focused approach. Steve insisted that no preliminary information should be given, issuing the simple and revealing instruction: "Ferdinand, let them ask questions and let us see what they want!"

It was thus made clear that we were not to act as the ones who "know" what to do; rather we should use the questions of the participants to develop a conversation about their issues and areas of interest, completely in the spirit of the solution-focused approach. In this seminar Steve de Shazer formulated the one decisive question, the only question which interested him in the context of consultation and was the focus for all his actions. He wrote this question on the flipchart. It read: "What does the client want?"

"A not too bad night"

Steve de Shazer had a particular brand of humour which he was able to express in his play on words, even in situations which for him were anything but humorous. Thus it was one of the most moving situations in my life when I visited Steve, shortly before his death in hospital. He had arrived at Vienna airport; during the flight he was obviously having extreme difficulties breathing, so upon landing he was brought straight to a doctor who had him taken immediately to hospital. While at the airport, Steve gave my phone number to the paramedics and asked them to call me. In laboured breaths, Steve told me his situation and that the doctor had had him hospitalised. I said that I would try to come immediately to assist him in communicating with the attending hospital staff.

When I arrived at the hospital, Steve was already in the intensive care unit, hooked up to various machines, and being supplied with oxygen. He could hardly breathe or talk, but was fully conscious. In the course of the next two hours Steve asked firstly, as usual, after my family and how my children were coming along and then asked me to cancel the planned Vienna seminar. He also asked me to inform Insoo Kim Berg, who was on her way to Malmö for a seminar.

When the doctors on duty signalled that I should now leave, since the situation was very stressful for the patient, I took my leave from Steve saying, "Have a good night, Steve!" to which he replied in his inimitable way: "This might not be a good night, but I hope it will be a not too bad night". Two hours later Steve de Shazer fell into a coma from which he would not wake.

These three episodes represent for me the quintessence of the solution-focused attitude, which I would like to summarise as follows:

1) The solution-focused approach strives to focus consistently on the expertise of the client in all stages of the consultation and to disregard as far as possible one's own perceptual concepts and hypotheses.
2) The solution-focused approach places considerable emphasis and thus makes great demands on the client's active participation, and

simultaneously requires of the therapist an unconditional, disciplined observation of, and focus on, the client. De Shazer put it in his own way in two striking statements:

- "If you work harder than your client, you become your own customer and then fire yourself!"
- "Do not think, observe!"

3) Notwithstanding all the difficulties, humour should be at the centre of the encounter and thus, in effect, offer a constantly fresh, alternative assessment of the situation to the initial evaluation, in accordance with the motto: "Putting difference to work".

Ferdinand Wolf Dr. phil. is a clinical psychologist and psychotherapist in Hornstein and Vienna, Austria. He is a teaching therapist for systemic family therapy of the Austrian Association for Systemic Therapy and Studies, Vienna, head of two counselling centres for early intervention in Vienna, a coach at the North German Institute for Brief Therapy, NIK, Bremen, at the Department of Systems experience in Prague and Kosice, and at the FH Campus, Vienna and at the Pedagogical University of Innsbruck.

Sabine Zehnder Schlapbach   Bern, Switzerland

After 10 years, Steve and Insoo are still ever-present!

Minutes of an Intervision meeting at Creathera, Bern

Bern, 18 February 2011

As usual, it is a diverse group that is meeting at the offices of Creathera in Bern. There is Ursula, the paediatric and adolescent psychiatrist, Christa, the educational therapist, Regula, the speech therapist, Ute, the paediatrician and youth psychologist, Alice, who is a remedial teacher and Felix and myself, Sabine, paediatricians and youth doctors.

The first case is reviewed. Madeleine, a 12 year-old girl in the fifth grade of primary school, is giving her teachers cause for concern. Her performance is inadequate, she neglects her duties, she lies, is evasive and, when confronted, always says "Ok, ok, I'll do it this time – promise". The single-parent African mother, who is repeatedly involved, also promises to motivate her daughter to participate. Unfortunately, these remain empty promises. The teachers and consultants are discouraged: countless conversations with the student, letters to her mother, a homework task book, checking by the mother (signing all tasks and learning tests), help with homework, reward systems, detentions, single or integrative remedial classes, none of these have changed anything about the situation. Nothing of the immense energy expended by the teachers seems to help.

"You're working too hard ..." Steve remarks. Indeed, the consultant seems to be investing more energy into finding a solution than Madeleine or her mother. What ideas does the girl herself have for a solution? And, above all, how does she view the whole situation?

Because that alone counts, as we know from the story of Princess Leonora in *Many Moons*, one of Insoo's favourite stories (Thurber & Sobodkin, 1943). Felix reminds us that the school, with all the demands it places on the kids, is basically a "coercive institution". In life, the only places one must go to are school and prison, he says ... everyone who works with children in the school context should be aware of that!

"What does Madeleine really want? And her mother? The teachers?" asks Ursula. Madeleine wants to be left alone, to have the time and opportunity to meet up with her friends. The mother wants cooperation and honesty from her daughter, and the stealing at home should also stop. The teacher expects completed tasks and homework and support for the student from her mother.

"Leading from one step behind" is now the motto, says Steve. This means that in the attempt to understand, the consultant places himself behind his client, considering the problem through their eyes and from this position, together with the client, changes the perspective in small steps. In this way solution options can be generated that until now have been elusive. "I'll do my best", Steve promises every client at the beginning.

"What is the smallest step towards a solution that makes a difference for the girl, the mother, the teacher?" Steve is heard to ask again. Insoo adds, "We should be able to hear the grass grow". We often succumb to the temptation to want to make great strides, but we should consider a step that is small enough that it can be attempted right away the next day.

Sabine pulls out a cartoon (opposite). Everyone laughs.

Alice said, "The mother and the teachers need to be appreciated". The mother always answers the phone in a very friendly manner and comes immediately to the school whenever asked to discuss matters. She also makes sure that her daughter gets to school on time. Insoo utters a loud "WOW". Everyone nods and knows exactly that "Working on what works" helps, not just in the classroom! Insoo continues, "How does she do it?" All the participants encourage each other to compliment themselves. This is more effective than direct compliments which, like a layer of sunscreen, remain on the surface and can be washed away.

.chluss-Strich von Oswald Huber

The psychiatrist is saying, "Well, if that isn't progress! For the first time in 6 years you have enough self-confidence to peek out from under the couch!"

Regula asks, "Could the communication be improved in any way? Was "solution-focused language" used and was the correct form of communication (written/spoken) selected? Were cultural aspects taken into account?" Black African cultures have an oral tradition. They take the spoken word more seriously than anything written because their cherished wisdom and history are passed down orally. If you want to be sure that people from this cultural circle regard information as important, it should be communicated in spoken form, e.g. by phone, or one could point out to them that in our culture, the written word is at least as important as, if not even more important than, the spoken word. Indeed, in this case, no written request had produced any effect at all.

"What can the teachers and consultants do to protect themselves from these distractions and annoyances and to continue their work with enthusiasm?" asks Ute. Christa says that on her way home every night she deliberately enters through the garden gate so that she can unload all the day's accumulated mental rubbish on the compost heap. Sabine smiles, "Since I always require a diagnosis when I settle up with the health insurance, I do my best to make this biologically-dynamically degradable ..." During annoying telephone calls, Insoo tells how she simply shakes out the telephone receiver over the floor! Or when she is dealing with families that start to fight each other during the consultation, she simply says "do this at home, without paying me".

In the second case study everyone gets involved in a similar manner, especially Steve and Insoo ... they don't miss a single Intervision meeting!

Concluding remarks

For ten years I was privileged to listen to countless quotes from Steve de Shazer or Insoo Kim Berg, with different voices in many different contexts. I also watched several videos of them working, and read their books. These were my first contacts with Steve and Insoo leading me to construct my reality, my own encounter with them, using my criteria.

In 2005 the time finally came when I was looking forward to the first real encounter with Steve in person. Unfortunately, it did not come about because of his unexpected death. The first planned meeting with Insoo in Zurich also did not take place since she passed away in early 2007.

Knowing that I would never meet either of them in the real world saddened me. But my experience of encounter through "not meeting" them, brings to life each saying of Steve and Insoo even more.

Reference

Thurber, J., & Sobodkin, L. (1943). *Many Moons*. San Diego: Harcourt Publishers Ltd; Reissue edition (1 Sept. 1987).

Sabine Zehnder Schlapbach MD is a specialist in child and adolescent medicine and a creative child therapist in private practice in Bern, Switzerland. She is an FMH with FA in medical hypnosis, SMSH and an employee of the inpatient child and youth services in Bern (Switzerland), as well as a founding member of Creathera, Bern and author of numerous publications.

Yvonne Dolan   Chicago, USA

Recipes from Milwaukee

I was looking for pictures of Steve and Insoo, but instead I found an old copy of Steve's Sicilian spaghetti recipe. Just today I was thinking of the times that Steve would FAX recipes to me and then call or send a very short email to find out if I had tried them in my kitchen that week! It then occurred to me that maybe you might like to include one or two recipes.

Steve liked to play what he called a "nice trick" on Insoo to get her to stop working at night and come downstairs. He would start cooking the sauce for this pasta and open the door near the stove (which was at the bottom of the stairs) so that the delicious small of garlic and tomatoes etc would waft through the air up to her upstairs office and lure her downstairs. I am sure it always worked! The smell of brownies worked too, so I include the recipe I often cooked for them.

Steve de Shazer's Sicilian Style Spaghetti Sauce

3 to 4 pounds fresh tomatoes, chopped, or 2 x 28oz cans diced tomatoes
6 cloves garlic, peeled and chopped
3 tablespoons capers, drained and rinsed
2 small boxes raisins
1 small bag slivered almonds
1 teaspoon hot pepper flakes
2 tablespoons fresh basil
3 pounds chicken thighs (about 8)

1. In a stock pot, heat olive oil for about 2 minutes.
2. Saute garlic, medium-low heat, for about 2 minutes.
3. Raise heat to medium, add tomatoes for about 10 minutes.

4. Add remaining ingredients except herbs for about 20 minutes.
5. Add basil, reduce to low heat.
6. In a large frying pan, heat olive oil for about 1 minute.
7. Add 4 thighs, skin side down, for about 5minutes, turn and fry the other side for about 5 minutes, turn and fry again for 3 minutes, then finally turn again and fry for 3 minutes. Remove to paper towel. Once cool, remove skin.
8. Repeat step 7 with the remaining thighs.
9. Add to sauce and simmer for about 20 minutes.

Serve over spaghetti type pasta.
Serves four very hungry therapists.

Yvonne's Brownies

During the years that I taught with Steve and Insoo in Milwaukee during their three week SF Summer Intensive Trainings at BFTC, I almost always brought a big pan of chocolate brownies for us to share with the participants. Brownies are very simple to make and they are one of the quintessential American desserts. Here is the recipe I used:

1 pound unsalted butter
1 pound plus 12 ounces semisweet or bittersweet chocolate*
6 ounces bitter (unsweetened) chocolate
6 large eggs
2 tablespoons pure vanilla extract
2 tablespoons instant coffee granules (I use decaffeinated or leave it out)
2 ¼ cups of sugar
1 ¼ cups all-purpose flour
1 tablespoon baking powder
1 teaspoon salt
3 cups chopped walnuts or pecans

---

* I used Vahlrona or Lindt but almost any kind will work!

Preheat the oven to 350 degrees. Butter and flour a 12 × 18 × 1" pan. Melt together the chocolates and butter in the micro-wave or over a low burner. Allow to cool slightly. In a large bowl combine the eggs, coffee granules, vanilla and sugar. Stir in the warm chocolate mixture. Gradually add the flour, baking powder, salt and walnuts, stirring until well combined. Pour into the prepared pan and bake for 35 minutes. Do NOT overbake! Allow to cool and then refrigerate before cutting into squares. Feeds a group of about 20 SF therapists. Freezes beautifully. Nuts may be omitted.

Acknowledgements

Our thanks go not only to Insoo Kim Berg and Steve de Shazer, but also to all the authors who have contributed their memories and stories to our collection, thus helping to create it.

We also thank Ms Balke-Schmidt of verlag modernes lernen Borgmann Publishers in Dortmund, who once again has made it possible for a broad readership to access the diversity, development and history of solution-focused practices.

We also wish to thank Ms Melanie Beron from the North German Institute for Brief Therapy, NIK Bremen, for the professional coordination of all contributions, Ms Gesa Möggenburg from Amsterdam for the competent translation of the manuscripts and Dr Christina Kotte from Freiburg for her helpful proof-reading and editing.

Acknowlededements for the English edition

We thank Dr Mark McKergow and Jenny Clarke of the Centre for Solutions Focus at Work (sfwork) in London for their help in putting together the English edition, and Dr Andrew Poulter for translating the German language contributions and materials into English. Kirsten Dierolf helped to translate a few tricky left-overs. Miles Bailey and his team at the Choir Press have done an excellent job of producing the book.

Abbreviations

We have adopted the abbreviations of the authors. The abbreviation SFBT is the common international acronym for solution focused brief therapy.

AAMFT American Association for Marriage and Family Therapy
BFTC Brief Family Therapy Center
EBTA European Brief Therapy Association
MRI Mental Research Institute, Palo Alto
SFBT Solution Focused Brief Therapy
SFBTA Solution Focused Brief Therapy Association of North America
SFCT Association for the Quality Development of Solution Focused Consulting and Training
SFT-L Solution Focused Mailing List and Network (Malmö)

Index

Also published by Solutions Books

If you have enjoyed this book, you may be interested in our other books on solution-focused and related practice.

Host: Six new ~~rules~~ roles of engagement for teams, organisations, communities and movements
Mark McKergow and Helen Bailey, ISBN 978–0954974985, £11.99 paperback (also on Kindle)

Miracle, Solution and System: Solution focused systemic structural constellations for therapy and organisational change
Insa Sparrer, ISBN 978–0954974954, £19.99 paperback

57 SF Activities for facilitators and consultants
Peter Röhrig and Jenny Clarke (editors), ISBN 978–0954974961, £29.99 hardback

Solutions Focus Working: 80 real-life lessons for successful organisational change
Mark McKergow and Jenny Clarke, ISBN 978–0954974947, £17.99 paperback

Team Coaching with the SolutionCircle: A practical guide to solution focused team development
Daniel Meier, ISBN 978–0954974913, £17.99 paperback (also on Kindle)

Positive Approaches to Change: Applications of Solutions Focus and Appreciative Inquiry at work
Mark McKergow and Jenny Clarke (editors), ISBN 978–0954974905, £13.99 paperback